An Hachette UK Company
www.hachette.co.uk

First published in the United Kingdom in 2020 by
Ilex, an imprint of
Octopus Publishing Group Ltd
Carmelite House
50 Victoria Embankment
London EC4Y 0DZ
www.octopusbooks.co.uk

Publisher: Alison Starling
Editorial Director: Zena Alkayat
Managing Editor: Rachel Silverlight
Editor: Jenny Dye
Editorial Assistant: Ellen Sandford O'Neill
Art Director: Ben Gardiner
Designer: Studio Polka
Photographer: Kim Lightbody
Stylist: Rachel Vere
Illustrator: Caitlin Keegan
Production Manager: Caroline Alberti

ISBN 978-1-78157-759-2

A CIP catalogue record for this book is available
from the British Library.

Printed and bound in China

10 9 8 7 6 5 4 3 2

YOU WILL BE ABLE TO KNIT BY THE END OF THIS BOOK

ROSIE FLETCHER

ilex

Introduction

Stitch and Technique Library

9 HOW TO USE THIS BOOK

12 YARN

Yarn weights	12
Fibre types	15
How to read a yarn band	16

19 KNITTING NEEDLES

Needle types	19
Needle sizes	20

22 OTHER EQUIPMENT

How to read a pattern	27
Holding your needles and yarn	28
Tying a slip knot	30
Casting on (CO)	31
Right and wrong sides	33
Knit (k)	34
Purl (p)	36
Increasing	38
Decreasing	41
Casting off (CO)	44
Stitch combinations	46
Working in the round	50
Colourwork	60
Slipped stitch patterns	62
Holding yarn double	63
Troubleshooting	64
Undoing your work	70
Tension	73
Finishing your work	74
Caring for your handknits	86

Projects

Chunky scarf   90
Reusable face wipes   94
Colourblock cushion cover   98
Mug cozy   102
Chunky hat with pompom   104
Doorstop   108
Tablet case   112
Baby shoes   116
Wrist warmers   118
Angle scarf   121
Mitred square blanket   128
Textured cushion cover   132
Slouchy beanie   136
Hot water bottle cover   140
Teddy   144
Shopping bag   148

154 FURTHER KNITTING

154 ABOUT THE AUTHOR

155 ACKNOWLEDGEMENTS

156 INDEX

Introduction

Welcome to the first steps of your knitting journey! This book is designed to give absolute beginners the help they'll need to take them from the very simplest scarf to more intricate projects that allow them to show off their new-found skills and create an array of homewares, accessories and items to gift or keep.

It can seem almost impossible that two sticks and some yarn can produce scarves, hats and so much more, but with a little patience and a little practise, you'll soon be knitting with confidence. More than that, this creative and calming craft can even change your life – it did mine!

Knitting has always been a comfort to me and has seen me through some of the toughest times. When I went through a long illness, being able to knit and create things made me feel that I could still do something useful and beautiful, even when my body could do so little. The rhythm of the needles and the flow of yarn is almost meditative – when you're trying to puzzle out a tricky pattern or a new technique, you can't think about anything else. When I recovered, my knitting became a full-time pursuit and I am now the owner of a wool and haberdashery shop in London. When I knitted my first very holey scarf I never thought that, just a few years later, I'd be embarking on a craft-focused career.

I love knitting. I carry a project everywhere I go and I get itchy fingers if I go too long without knitting a few rows. I hope you enjoy this book and learning to knit from it, and that you too will catch the bug. Getting to share my love of knitting is my favourite part of my job. I firmly believe that anyone can knit – and everyone should.

How to use this book

The book is divided into two parts: a 'stitch and technique library' that explains the skills you need to master and a collection of project patterns that will help you to put those skills into practice. If knitting is totally new to you, try out the techniques from the first half of the book before tackling the projects. This will give you a chance to build your confidence and get a little practise before committing to a whole pattern. Those of you who have had a go at knitting already could dip into the projects and refer to the techniques as and when you need them.

Knitting can seem pretty daunting at first, but don't be put off – a little practise goes a long way. The key to developing consistently and quickly is not to try to run before you can walk – or in other words, don't try to knit in the round before you can purl! With that in mind, the project patterns in this book are designed to get progressively more complex, so while you might want to try the Shopping Bag on page 148 straight away, you might find it a little overwhelming if you haven't followed a pattern before. It's better to start with the Chunky Scarf pattern on page 90, which uses the very basic building blocks of knitting to make a cozy neck warmer, and then continue from there.

Don't be dispirited if your first attempts don't look exactly like the pattern – everyone's first bit of knitting looks a little 'homemade' and you'll soon get the hang of it.

And once you do, you'll find that knitting patterns are a lot like recipes: you need to follow the instructions, but you can still add your own touches. If you don't want to knit the Tablet Case (page 112) in stripes, do it in a solid colour; and if you want to turn the Colourblock Cushion Cover (page 98) into a tote bag, you should do so! Knitting is about being creative and I hope this book gives you the skills and confidence you need to fall in love with this brilliant craft.

'The rhythm of the
needles and the flow of
yarn is almost meditative
– when you're trying
out a pattern or a new
technique, you can't think
about anything else.'

Yarn

Choosing a beautiful yarn is one of the most enjoyable parts of embarking on a new project. But understanding yarn – and matching the right yarn to a project – is essential. The same pattern knitted in two different yarns can have very different outcomes.

YARN WEIGHTS

Yarn comes in different 'weights' – this refers to the thickness of the yarn, not how much it actually weighs. If you're substituting one yarn for another, the most important thing to match is the weight of the yarn – a pattern for a very thin yarn knitted in a thick yarn will come out very dense and tough. So, if a pattern calls for a specific yarn that you can't find, check its weight and find an alternative in the same weight.

There are two main systems of naming yarn weights, either with an actual name, such as 'superfine' (the names vary in the UK, US and Australia), or with a number. To make things a touch simpler, the two standard naming conventions do correspond to one another:

COMMON NAMES	PLY
Laceweight	2 ply
Superfine / Fingering	4 ply
Sport	5 ply
DK / Light Worsted	8 ply
Aran / Worsted	10 ply
Chunky / Bulky	12 ply
Super Chunky / Super Bulky	14 ply

YARN

INTRODUCTION

FIBRE TYPES

When it comes to selecting a yarn, not only do you get to pick the exact colour you want, but there are lots of different fibres and textures to choose from, too.

Although they are sometimes used interchangeably, 'yarn' and 'wool' aren't quite the same thing. Yarn refers to any material you knit with, whereas wool is specifically made from sheep fleece.

All the patterns in this book suggest specific yarns to use. While you don't have to buy those exact ones, you'll want a fairly close match in fibre type and weight for a successful knit.

Here are some of the yarn fibre types you'll encounter:

WOOL

Wool is the quintessential fibre for yarn, but the humble sheep produces a wide range of wools. Yarn from merino sheep – commonly referred to as just 'merino' – is famed for its softness, thanks to the fineness of the fleece. At the other end of the scale, the wool used in traditional Icelandic jumpers seems very rough and scratchy before it's knitted, but relaxes to become warm, durable and much more wearable once it's been knitted and washed. Wool is warm yet breathable, hard-wearing yet cozy. Some wools, labelled superwash, are treated to be machine washable – but take care when washing your woollens, as you don't want to spend all that time on a project just for it to shrink in the washing machine.

ALPACA

Alpaca are the smaller, cuter sibling of the llama and their fleece is super soft. Alpaca yarn can be more expensive than wool, so it's often sold in a blend of the two to get the benefits of this soft yet strong fleece without the high price tag. It's also great for people who are allergic to the lanolin in sheep's wool, as alpaca doesn't contain any.

COTTON AND LINEN

If you'd rather not use animal fibres in your knitting, cotton and linen make for a great vegan alternative. Cotton and linen derive from plants and, while they don't have the bounce of wool, they have a beautiful drape and the strength of the yarn makes it perfect for homewares.

ACRYLIC

Acrylic yarns need not be as maligned as they sometimes are. Some artificial yarns rival merino for their softness, while their ability to withstand a washing machine shouldn't go unappreciated. Even the most ardent devotees of handspun, natural yarns need some hard-wearing acrylic in their sock yarns – otherwise your socks would fall apart after only a few wears. Acrylic can often be cheaper than natural fibres, so it makes a great starting place for new knitters.

HOW TO READ A YARN BAND

All yarn comes with a paper band around it. Your instinct might be to throw it away as soon as you've opened it, but these yarn bands are full of useful information.

Yarn name and brand
First, the band will tell you the name of the yarn brand and of that particular yarn. It might not seem important, but if you ever want to try and find more of the same yarn, you'll need to know what it was called.

Colour and dye lot
There will also be a specific colour and dye lot – these will be followed by numbers. Each colour of yarn has a code number attached to it and a company will give each batch of yarn dyed in that colour a dye lot number. If you're hunting for a colour match, the colour number should be enough, but if you need a lot of yarn in one go, try to get them all from the same dye lot, just in case there are differences between batches.

Fibre type
The band will tell you what the fibre content is, so you know whether you're knitting with yarn that is pure wool, acrylic or a mix of fibres.

Ball weight and length
It will also tell you the weight of the ball (not to be confused with the weight of the yarn itself). Yarn is usually sold in 50g and 100g balls. It will also tell you how many metres or yards of yarn there are in the ball.

Gauge
The gauge section might look technical at first, but it is useful for knowing how the yarn will look when knitted (see page 73). It will tell you how many stitches and how many rows fit in a 10cm (4in) square when the yarn is knitted using the recommended size of needle. All yarns have a recommended needle size, but you may want to use slightly bigger or smaller ones to give a tighter or looser fabric.

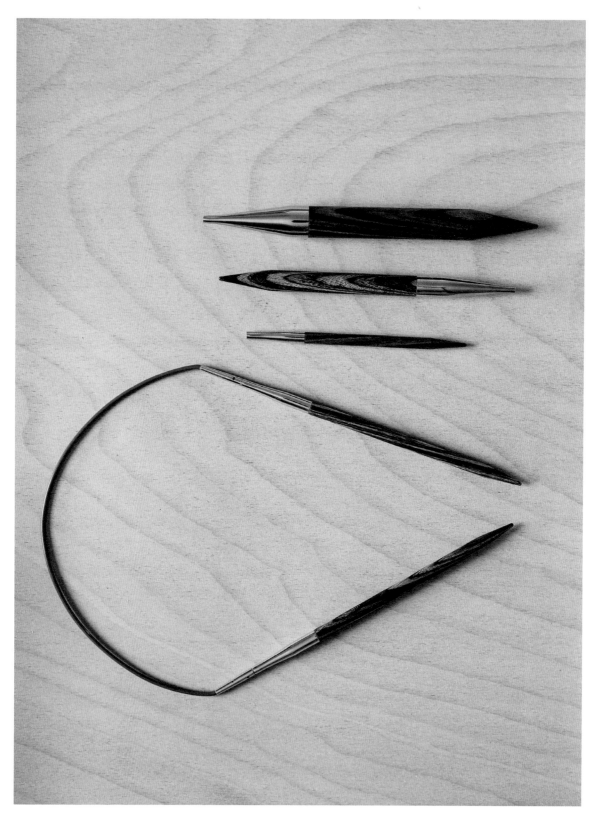

INTRODUCTION

Knitting needles

After you've selected the right yarn, you'll need knitting needles. Needles come in a range of sizes and styles and experienced knitters will tell you exactly what kind they prefer: bamboo or aluminium, straight or circular. There is no right answer, so simply experiment and find what feels comfortable for you.

NEEDLE TYPES

Straight needles
Picture knitting and you'll almost certainly envisage a pair of straight knitting needles. These are the place to start for beginners, as you can clearly see how the two needles interact with each other. Straight needles come in different lengths – some people like really long needles, some people find them cumbersome. Start with needles around 25cm (10in) or 30cm (12in) long and you'll get a feel for what you like.

Circular needles
There are also circular needles. These look like two short straight needles joined by a flexible cable. They are used for knitting in the round (see page 50) where your knitting creates a tube rather than a flat piece of fabric. Rather than work the stitches back and forth across the fabric, you work round and round. These also come in different lengths: 40cm (16 in) needles are the place to start for making a hat.

Double-pointed needles
You can also use double-pointed needles for knitting in the round. These are sets of four or five shorter needles with points on each end. They can knit smaller circumferences than circular needles.

NEEDLE SIZES

The most important thing about needles is the size you use – this refers to the diameter or 'thickness' rather than the length. Your pattern will always tell you what size you need, and this will correspond to the yarn being used. Fine yarns call for thinner needles and chunky yarns need thicker needles – the size of the knitting needle determines the size of the stitch and you can't get really thick yarn through a really small stitch.

As with yarn weights, there are several systems for naming needle sizes. This book uses metric sizes throughout, with US sizes in brackets. This handy chart should help:

METRIC SIZES	IMPERIAL	US
2mm	14	0
2.25mm	13	1
2.75mm	12	2
3mm	11	–
3.25mm	10	3
3.5mm	–	4
3.75mm	9	5
4mm	8	6
4.5mm	7	7
5mm	6	8
5.5mm	5	9
6mm	4	10
6.5mm	3	10.5
7mm	2	–
7.5mm	1	–
8mm	0	11
9mm	00	13
10mm	000	15
12mm	–	17

KNITTING NEEDLES

Other equipment

It's easy to get overwhelmed by all the extra pieces of equipment (often referred to as 'notions') available to knitters, but you don't need to panic. There are a few of these tools that are helpful to the new knitter.

Stitch markers
These are small rings that slide onto your needles between stitches to mark where you are in a pattern. They are really useful, especially if you have a lot of stitches to keep track of. When you encounter one, slip it from the left needle to the right without knitting it. They also make really cute gifts for knitters who love something sparkly to decorate their works in progress!

Row counters
If you keep losing track of how far you've got through a pattern, slide a row counter on the end of one of your needles. Each time you knit a row, twist it round once and you'll never have to struggle to count your rows again!

Tapestry needle
A blunt tapestry or large-eyed sewing needle comes in handy right at the end of your project. Using a blunt needle to sew in the ends of your work prevents you from splitting your yarn, so you can achieve a neat finish. Invest in several – these have a tendency to get lost. You may also want a thimble to protect your finger while sewing.

Tension measuring tool
You may think you know how long a hat should be, but without a tension measuring tool, you're at risk of the brim of your beanie coming down past your chin.

Dressmaker pins
For handknits knitted in sections and then joined together, T-shaped pins (the T bars stop the pins slipping from through the stitches) are useful for holding the pieces in place as they are joined.

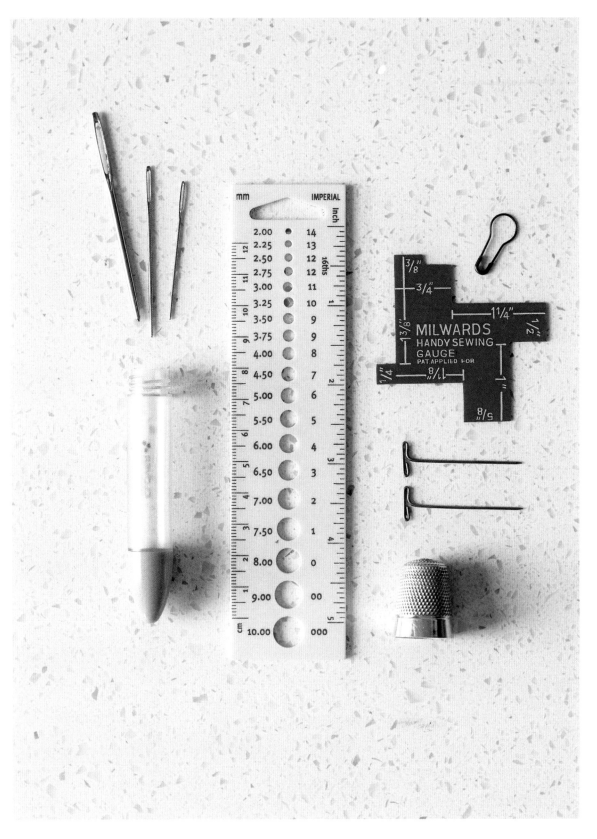

Stitch and

Technique Library

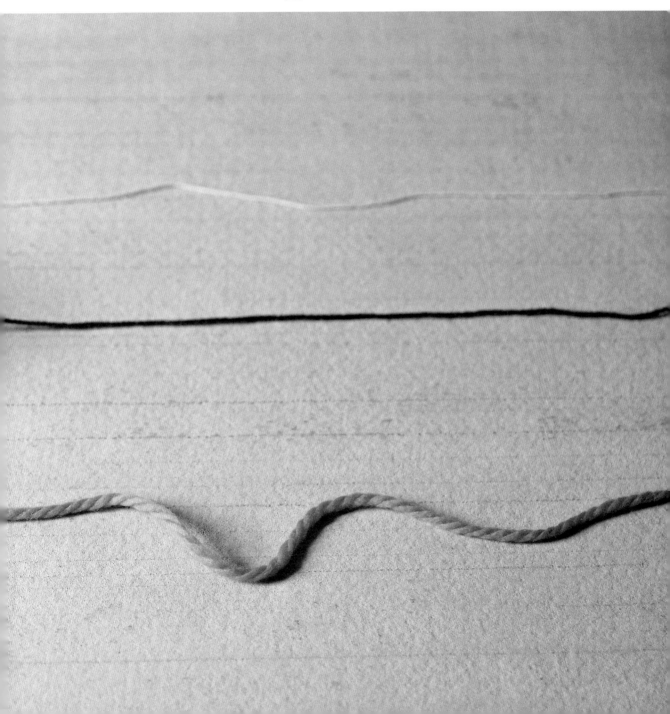

How to read a pattern

Knitting patterns can look indecipherable at first glance, but there's no reason to be scared of them. No matter what you're making, from your first scarf to a cabled jumper, your pattern will have a standard format to make things clear.

Just as a recipe starts with a list of ingredients, a pattern will begin by telling you the equipment you need. It might suggest a specific yarn to use or only the amount and weight of yarn. It will tell you which needles to use so you don't need to work it out for yourself.

Next, the method will be divided into steps to follow in order: it's helpful to read the whole pattern through first, so that you understand the overall construction of a project.

Pattern instructions are abbreviated. For example, knit four stitches becomes 'k4'. Patterns with more complex instructions will often include a list of abbreviations. If they are in square brackets, you should repeat them as many times as instructed. These are some of the abbreviations and instructions you're most likely to encounter:

STITCH NAME	ABBREVIATION
knit	k
purl	p
stitches	st
cast on / cast off	CO
bind off (in US patterns)	BO
knit 2 stitches together	k2tog
slip, slip, knit	ssk
make 1 stitch	m1
yarn over needle	yon

Holding your needles and yarn

There are two knitting needles – one for each hand. There's no right way to hold your needles. Some knitters hold theirs from underneath like a pen, others from on top like a knife. Whatever makes knitting easy and comfortable for you is fine.

There are two common styles of holding yarn – English and continental. English knitters (found the world over!) hold their yarn in their right hand and 'throw' it around their needles. Continental knitters hold their yarn in their left hand and 'pick up' the yarn with the tip of the right-hand needle. This book uses English knitting, with additional instructions, where appropriate, for continental knitting.

The important thing to consider when holding your yarn is that there needs to be some tension in it. You don't need to yank it – these are stitches, not knots – but you do need to keep your stitches from being too loose. Otherwise they become baggy and you lose your stitch definition. Some knitters run their yarn between their fingers to keep it taut. Others just give their yarn a gentle tug as they make each stitch. With practise you will find which method works for you and gives you the most consistent tension across your knitting.

ENGLISH STYLE

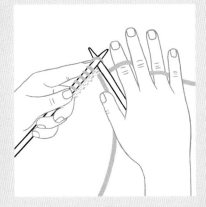 

Holding yarn
English knitters hold the working yarn in their right hand, often running it between their fingers to keep the tension.

Holding needles
They then wrap the working yarn around the right needle as though 'throwing it' around to create a stitch.

CONTINENTAL STYLE

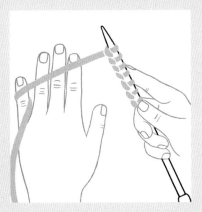 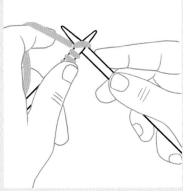

Holding yarn
Continental knitters hold the working yarn in their left hand – some keep the tension by wrapping it around their pinkie, others use their index finger, and some people use both fingers.

Holding needles
They can then just 'pick up' the yarn with their right needle to create a new stitch.

Tying a slip knot

The proper way to attach your yarn to your knitting needle is with a slip knot.

1.
Pull out a small length of yarn from the ball. Leaving a short tail of about 10cm (4in), create a loop by laying the short tail over the top of your working yarn. The working yarn is attached to the ball of yarn – the tail is the short end left over.

Then, reach through that loop…

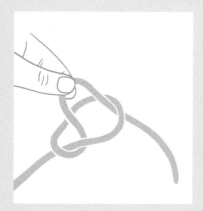

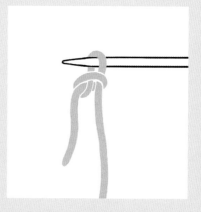

2.
…and pull a loop of the tail through it.

3.
Pull the working yarn tight around that loop.

4.
Insert your needle through the loop you have made and pull the working yarn to tighten. This is a slip knot – and your first stitch.

Casting on (CO)

For any project, you first need to set up the number of stitches you'll be starting with. This is called casting on. It is abbreviated in patterns to 'CO' followed by a number. For example, 'CO10' would mean 'cast on 10 stitches'.

There are lots of different methods for casting on your stitches – this is the easiest as it is very similar to the knit stitch. It's called the 'knitting on' method.

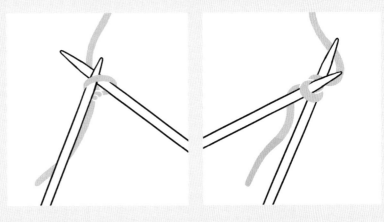

1.
Hold the needle with the slip knot in your left hand. Hold the empty needle in your right hand and insert the tip into the slip knot on the left needle, going from left to right and behind the left needle.

2.
With the right needle behind the left, wrap your working yarn anti-clockwise around the right needle, so that it is between the two needles.

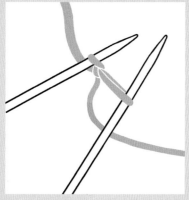 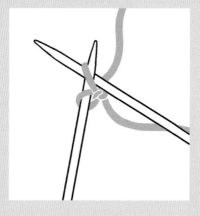 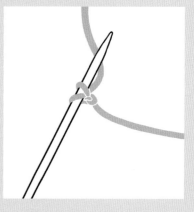

3.
Use the right needle to pull this yarn through the stitch on your left needle, creating a new stitch on the right needle.

4.
Put this stitch onto the left needle by inserting the left needle into the front of the stitch, going from left to right.

5.
Pull the right needle out of the stitch. Give the working yarn a tug to make it snug but not too tight.

   The stitch you have just made is now the second stitch on the left needle – repeat the process until you have the right number of stitches on your needle. Remember, the slip knot counts as the first stitch.

Right and wrong sides

Before you go on to master the stitches described on the following pages, it's worth understanding the concept of a 'row'. Each line of stitches across your needle is called a row. You complete a row by working every stitch on the left needle, transferring the new stitches to your right needle as you go. When you've emptied your left needle of stitches, you switch the needles over – turning your work so that the points of the needles are towards each other with the empty needle in your right hand – and work your next row.

Because you are going back and forth, turning your work, your knitting has a 'right side' and a 'wrong side', abbreviated in patterns to 'RS' and 'WS'.

You can tell the work is turning back and forth by watching the short tail left over from casting on. It will hang on either the bottom left or the bottom right depending on which side you're working. When you knit every row, both sides will look the same, but when you get to purling, you will see a difference.

Knit (k)

The knit stitch is the foundation of all stitches in knitting
– with this under your belt, you're well on your way to
mastering every other knitting technique. It's abbreviated
in patterns as 'k', usually followed by a number. For
example, 'k10' would mean 'knit 10 stitches'.

   Once you've cast on the right number of stitches for
your project, you're ready to start knitting them. Hold the
needle with the cast-on stitches in your left hand – you'll
work them with your right-hand needle.

  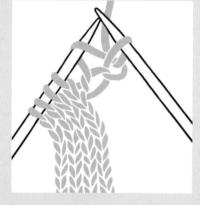

1.
Insert the tip of your right
needle into the front of the first
stitch on your left needle, going
from left to right and behind the
left needle.

2.
With your right needle behind
the left, wrap the yarn anti-
clockwise around the right
needle, so that it is between
the two needles.

3.
Use the right needle to pull this
yarn through, creating a new
stitch on the right needle.

4.
Slide the original stitch off the left needle.

5.
Pull the working yarn gently so that the stitch fits snugly on your right needle. You can now work the next stitch on your left needle.

Purl (p)

Purling is another integral part of knitting and is used in combination with the knit stitch to make different textures and designs. It is abbreviated in patterns as 'p' and, like the knit stitch, is followed by a number to tell you how many stitches you should purl. So 'p4' would mean 'purl 4 stitches'.

The purl stitch creates the 'wrong side' view of a knit stitch on the right side of your work (see page 33). By alternating knit rows on the right side of your work and purl rows on the wrong side, your finished item has only 'right sides' of knit stitches on the right side of the work. This creates a fabric that is smooth on the right side and bumpy on the wrong side.

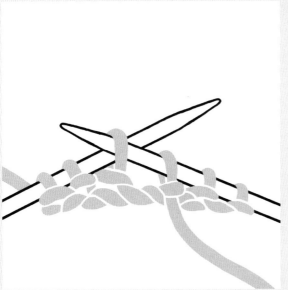

1.
Make sure that the working yarn is at the front of the work, taking care not to wrap it around either needle.

Insert your right needle into the front of the next stitch of your left needle, from right to left.

2.
Wrap the yarn anti-clockwise around the right needle and pull taut.

3.
Use the right needle to pull the yarn through the stitch on the left needle, creating a new stitch.

4.
Slide the original stitch off the left needle. Gently pull the working yarn so that the stitch fits snugly.

Increasing

To add shaping to your knitting, you can change the number of stitches in your rows. There are several different ways to increase the number of stitches you're working with, as detailed here.

YARN OVER NEEDLE (yon)
The simplest way to increase stitches is the yarn over needle technique. This increase creates a hole (or 'eyelet') where it was made – it's often used in lacey patterns or for decorative increases.

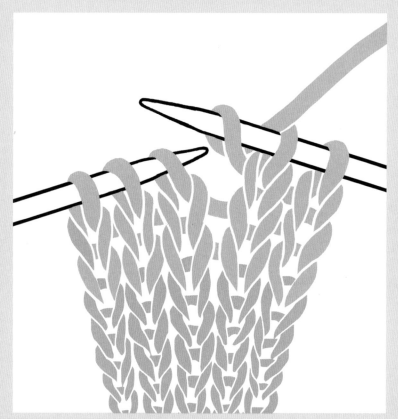

1.
Wrap the yarn anti-clockwise over your right needle – as you do when creating an actual stitch – and bring the yarn to the back of your work (or to the front if you are purling).

2.
With this extra 'stitch' on the right needle, work the next stitch as normal and continue to the end of the row.

3.
On the next row, treat the yarn over you created as though it were a normal stitch.

MAKE 1 (m1)

This increase uses the gap between two stitches and is created by lifting the yarn that runs between them.

1.
Knit at least one stitch and hold your needles slightly apart, so you can see the yarn that runs horizontally between the stitches.

With your left needle, go underneath this yarn from the front, lifting it up onto your left needle.

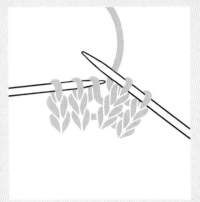 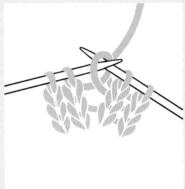

2.
Put your right needle into the back of this stitch, going from right to left.

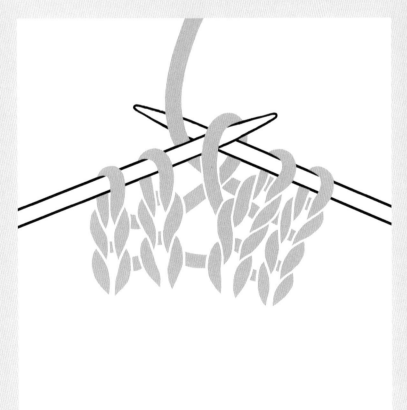

3.
Knit the stitch as usual, wrapping your working yarn around the right needle, pulling it through, and then slipping the lifted stitch off the left needle.

By knitting the lifted stitch through the back, it twists and becomes tighter and therefore less noticeable.

KNIT FRONT AND BACK (kfb)

This method of increasing stitches creates two stitches out of one, rather than making a new stitch between two existing stitches. It keeps the increase tight, as it doesn't pull on the gaps between stitches.

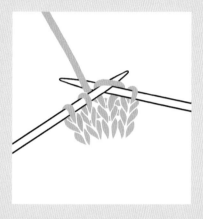

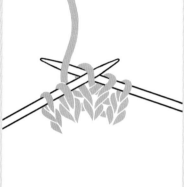

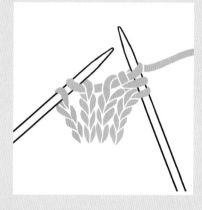

1.
Knit into the front of a stitch as normal, but do not slip the stitch off your left needle.

2.
Put your right needle back into the same stitch on the left needle, but this time insert it through the back of the loop, from right to left.

3.
Knit this stitch, wrapping your yarn around the right needle and pulling it through. Slip the stitch off the left needle.

Decreasing

Decreasing is also used to shape your knitting – it's what makes a hat hat-shaped, rather than just a straight tube.

KNIT TWO TOGETHER (k2tog)

The easiest way to decrease your number of stitches is to knit two together. The name is pretty self-explanatory – instead of just knitting one stitch, you knit two stitches from your left needle to only make one stitch on your right. It's abbreviated in patterns as k2tog. You can also purl two together (p2tog) in exactly the same manner – put your right needle through two stitches rather than one and work them together.

Knitting two stitches together is very similar to knitting one stitch:

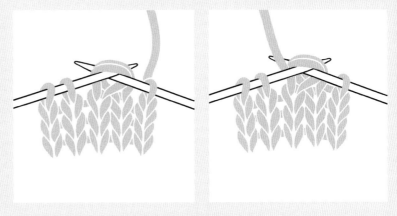

1.
Insert the tip of your right needle into the front of the second stitch on your left needle and continue into the front of the first stitch.

2.
Work as you would a normal knit stitch. Finish by slipping both stitches off your left needle.

SLIP SLIP KNIT (ssk)

When you knit two stitches together, you effectively stack those two stitches on top of each other. Knitting two stitches together puts the second stitch from your left needle on top, so the decrease appears to lean to the right. To put the first stitch on top and create a left-leaning decrease, you can use a slip slip knit, abbreviated to 'ssk'.

1.
Put your right needle into the first stitch as though you are about to knit it – but stop there. Slide the left needle out of that stitch – this is called a slip stitch, transferring a stitch from the left to the right needle without working it.

   Repeat for the next stitch on the left needle. Slide it off the left and onto the right needle. You now have two stitches on your right needle.

2.
Put the left needle into both these stitches, going from left to right, in front of the right needle.

   Wrap your yarn clockwise and work as you would a normal knit stitch, finishing by slipping both stitches off your left needle.

PASS SLIPPED STITCH OVER (psso)

Another way to decrease using slipped stitches is pass slipped stitch over or 'psso'. The slipped stitch in this is slightly different as it is slipped purlwise, as though you were about to purl it.

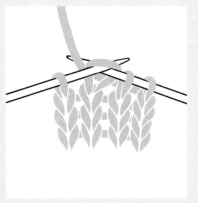 

1.
With the yarn behind your work, put the right needle in the front of the first stitch on your left needle from right to left. Slip the left needle out of this stitch.

Knit the next stitch on your left needle as normal, with the right needle going from left to right.

2.
Next, put the left needle inside the slipped stitch on the right needle. Lift this up and over the knitted stitch to its left. You've now decreased one stitch.

Casting off (CO)

Without the needle to hold them in place, stitches unravel. To finish your project and keep those stitches in place, you need to 'cast off' your work. This is abbreviated to 'CO' and it's the very last instruction in a pattern. In American patterns, this is known as 'binding off' and abbreviated to 'BO'.

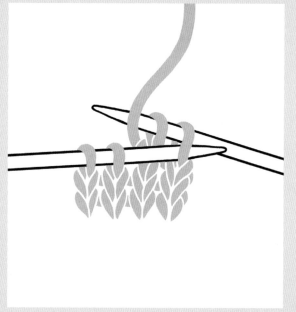

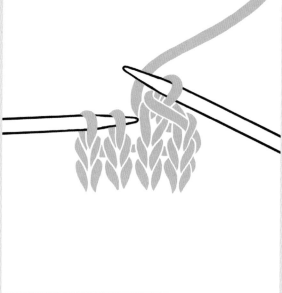

1.
Knit the first two stitches in your row as usual. Then insert the left needle into the first stitch you worked.

2.
Lift that stitch up and over the second stitch, leaving you with one stitch on your right needle.

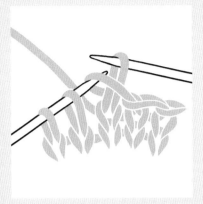 

3.
Knit the next stitch on your left needle as usual and then repeat step 2, lifting the previous stitch on your right needle over.

4.
Repeat this until you have one stitch left on your right needle. Cut the yarn, leaving a 15cm (6in) tail, thread this through your last stitch and pull tight.

KNITWISE VS PURLWISE / EDGES
Depending on the stitches you've been knitting, you will either need to cast off knitwise, purlwise, or a mix of the two – the pattern will always tell you which one you need.

Knitwise
The illustrations on these two pages show you how to cast off knitwise – you can see that the yarn is always behind the needles.

Purlwise
To cast off purlwise, purl the first two stitches and, using the left needle, lift the first stitch over the second, leaving you with one stitch on the needle. Then purl the next stitch and repeat. The yarn would always be in front.

Cast-off edges
Cast-off edges can often end up tighter than the rest of your knitting, so don't pull these stitches too tight when you're working them. If you find that your cast-off edge is still too tight, cast off with a bigger needle than the one you used in your project. This will make the stitches larger and give them more room to stretch.

Stitch combinations

You can create different fabrics and patterns depending on how you combine knit and purl stitches. The two main types are called 'garter stitch' and 'stocking stitch'. Although they are called stitches, they are created by combining knit and purl stitches.

GARTER STITCH

Garter stitch is the simplest fabric to create. It is made by working only knit stitches on every row. It makes for a very stable fabric that doesn't roll inwards at the edges.

STOCKING STITCH

Stocking stitch is made by alternating knit and purl rows. This creates the smooth rows of 'Vs' on the right side of the fabric that you'll recognize not just from commercial knitwear, but also from any knitted fabric such as the jersey in t-shirts or tights.

With all knit stitches on one side of the fabric – because purl stitches make the reverse of a knit stitch – stocking stitch naturally rolls in on itself. To get stocking stitch to lie flat, it needs a border of either garter stitch or ribbed stitches.

RIBBING

Ribbing is often found on cuffs, collars, the bottom of jumpers and the rims of hats. It's stretchy and elastic and stops stocking stitch curling in on itself. Ribbing looks the same on the right side as it does on the wrong side.

It is made by alternating knit and purl stitches and can be done in different combinations. For example, you can alternate between one knit and one purl stitch, or two knit and two purl, or even three knit and one purl. Your pattern will abbreviate these instructions to 'k1, p1', or 'k2, p2' or 'k3, p1' respectively.

MOSS STITCH

Moss stitch is created by working k1, p1 on the right side of your work and p1, k1 on the wrong side (assuming you have an even number of stitches on each row). It creates a chequerboard effect.

Working in the round

So far, you've been knitting flat pieces of fabric where the rows of knitting zigzag back and forth on top of each other. To create tubular pieces of knitting – that'll eventually lead you to knitting sleeves and socks – you work in the round and your rows spiral on top of each other.

Knitting in the round can look daunting at first, but it is really simple once you get going – and it saves a whole load of sewing up at the end of a project. It requires slightly different needles from those you've been using so far – either circular needles or double-pointed needles (dpn); see page 19 for more on these needles.

CIRCULAR NEEDLES

1.
Circular needles are held in exactly the same way as a pair of straight needles. You can still think of having a left needle and a right needle, even though they're connected.

Cast on the correct number of stitches for your pattern as normal and spread them evenly along your circular needle. The stitches should comfortably reach all the way along the cable and onto the right-hand needle.

2.

Make sure the cast-on stitches aren't twisting or spiralling around your needle – otherwise your knitting project will end up with twists and spirals that you won't be able to correct later.

    The illustration on the left shows the stitches twisted on the right-hand needle – you want to avoid this. The image on the right shows all the stitches neatly lying flat, as they should be.

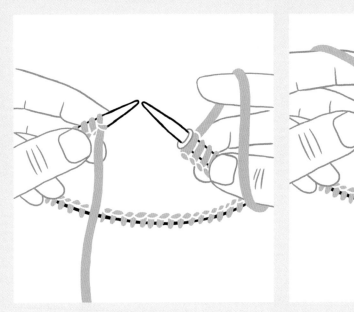

3a. <u>English style</u>

When you've finished casting on, switch the needles round in your hands so that the very first stitch you cast on is at the top of the left-hand needle. Your working yarn (and the last stitch you cast on) is at the top of your right-hand needle.

It can be hard to tell where the beginning and end of your row is when you're knitting in the round. Pop a stitch marker onto your right-hand needle above your last cast-on stitch to mark the beginning of the round.

3b. <u>Continental style</u>

The illustration above shows the same switch from left hand to right hand as 3a, but demonstrates where the working yarn will be if you are knitting in the continental style.

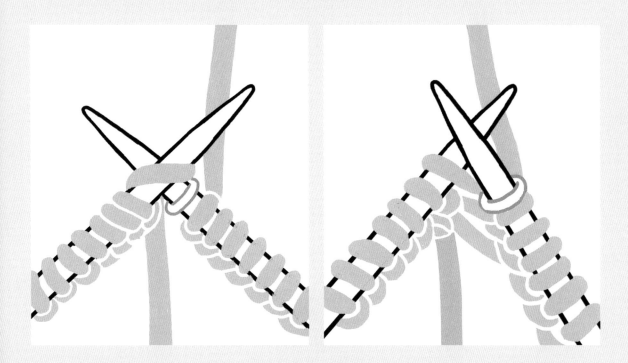

4.
Insert the tip of the right needle into the stitch on your left needle – that's the very first stitch you cast on – and knit it as normal.

5.
Continue working your way along the left-hand needle. You might need to pull your stitches clockwise along the cable as you go so that they reach round to the top of the left-hand needle.

When you reach your stitch marker, you have knitted one row (sometimes called 'one round' when you knit in the round). Slip your stitch marker from the left needle to the right needle and continue knitting from the left needle onto the right.

Because you aren't turning your work, you never knit on the wrong side when you knit in the round. That way, you can build up rows and rows of stocking stitch (see page 47) without ever purling.

When you have finished your work, cast off as normal. Cut the yarn and sew the yarn tail in in the direction you were knitting so that the cast-off edge is smooth.

DOUBLE-POINTED NEEDLES

Using a set of four double-pointed needles works in a very similar manner to knitting in the round on circular needles. Instead of creating a circle of knitting with a flexible cable joining two needles, the multiple needles create a jointed needle. They're useful for knitting very small circumferences in the round.

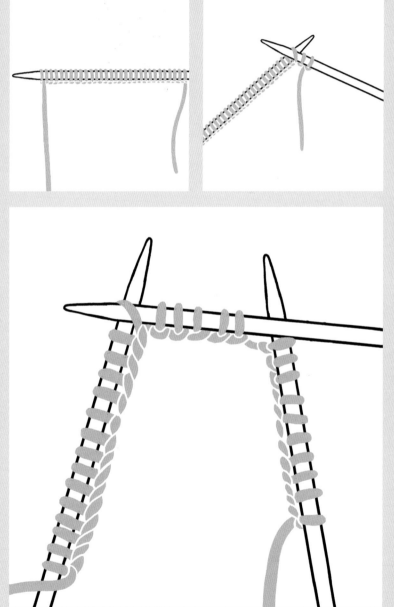

1.
Cast on your stitches onto one of the needles, making sure the stitches don't slip off the other end of the needle!

2.
Now you need to divide the stitches evenly across three of your needles. Start by slipping a third of the stitches purlwise (put your right needle into the stitch as though you were going to purl it) onto one of your empty knitting needles...

3.
...and then slip the next third onto a third needle, again slipping them purlwise.

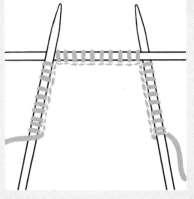

4.
You'll now need to check that your stitches aren't twisting around your needles. Be extra sure that the stitches are lying flat at the joins between your needles.

5.
Pick up your needles and hold them in a 'U' shape, so that the first cast-on stitch is top left and the working yarn is top right.

6.
Pick up your fourth and final needle and insert it into the first stitch on your left-hand needle. Use the working yarn to knit this stitch onto the new needle.

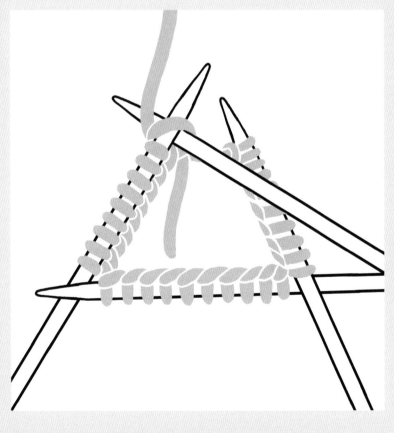

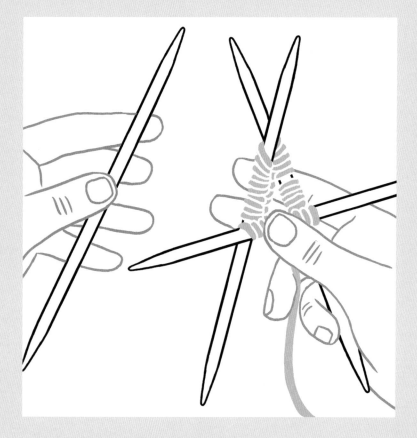

7.
Continue working along the needle on the left, knitting the cast-on stitches onto your fourth needle.

Once the first needle is empty of stitches, it becomes your new working needle. Continue knitting anti-clockwise around your needles, changing the working needle every time one empties.

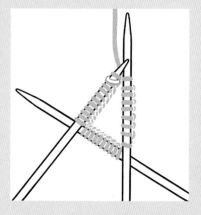

8.
At the start of your work, you'll be able to use the cast-on tail to tell where the round starts. As you move away from it, it can be a bit harder to follow. To use a stitch marker, you'll need to move the last stitch of the round onto the same needle as the first stitch, so that your stitch marker doesn't slip right off the end of the needle.

TROUBLESHOOTING KNITTING IN THE ROUND

Once you get the hang of knitting in the round, you may become a total convert and start whipping up hats every weekend. Here are some helpful tips to make it easier:

Gapping

When you get to the end of your first round, you may find that a gap has developed between your first and last stitches with a longer length of yarn between them. This is just because your first round isn't finished, so that last cast-on stitch is pulling away from its neighbour. When you knit over this gap, give your yarn a good tug to pull it tight – within a couple of rows, that gap will disappear.

Laddering

When you're working with double-pointed needles, you might find that you develop a 'ladder' of loose stitches that shows where your needles met. Make sure you pull the stitches at each end of your needle extra tight to stop this happening.

Switching needles

If you're knitting a hat in the round and start on circular needles, you'll need to switch to double-pointed needles to knit the crown as circular needles aren't suited to small circumferences. To switch, hold one double-pointed needle in your right hand and knit a third of the round onto it. Pick up another double-pointed needle and knit the next third on, then knit the last third onto another double-pointed needle. You can now pick up your fourth double-pointed needle and work the remaining portion of the hat on double points.

A ribbed pattern

When you're knitting something with a rib, cast off in that rib pattern – knit the knit stitches and purl the purl stitches before you slip the previous stitch over them. That will keep the edge as stretchy as the rest of the rib.

'It can seem impossible
that two sticks and
some yarn can produce
scarves, hats and so much
more, but with a little
practise, you'll be knitting
with confidence.'

Colourwork

Once you've got the hang of knitting, you'll want to start to experiment. Colour is an easy way to make a bright and bold statement. You can eventually move on to doing intricate stranded and Fair Isle patterns, but don't overlook the humble stripe for its playfulness and versatility.

STARTING A NEW COLOUR

Changing colours in your knitting is super simple and effective and is used in lots of the patterns in this book to show off your beginner's skills with maximum impact.

This is also how you can join a second ball of yarn into your work when the first runs out in the middle of a scarf. It's also used to change colour for maximum impact in the Colourblock Cushion Cover (see page 98).

1. Begin your knitting as you would any other project and knit up to the row in which you want to change colour. If you're knitting garter stitch (knit every row), change colour at the start of a right-side row – otherwise your stripe won't make a sharp line.

2. At the start of your next row, cut the first yarn, leaving a 15cm (6in) tail. Still holding onto this tail, put the right needle into the first stitch as usual but loop the new yarn colour around your right needle, leaving a 15cm (6in) tail.

3. Keeping hold of both yarns stops the original stitch from getting too loose. If you find that the first stitch in the new colour is getting loose, gently pull on both tails after you have knitted further along the row.

4. And that's it! Complete the rest of the row as usual.

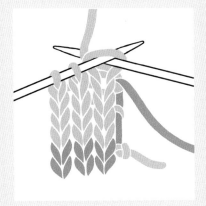

ALTERNATING COLOURS

If you're knitting narrow stripes and don't want to weave in a lot of ends (see page 80), you can change colours without cutting the original yarn. You can use this stripe effect for evenly spaced stripes or play around with different widths of stripes. This only works if you are doing stripes in even numbers of rows, as you need to knit two rows to get back to where your yarns are joined.

1. Knit to where you want to change colour and, as described opposite, begin knitting with the new colour – but don't cut the original colour yarn. Leave the ball hanging from your work.

2. When you've knitted two rows, you'll come back to where the original yarn is still attached. Twist both yarns around each other once and continue knitting with whichever of the colours you want to use next, either switching back to the original or continuing with the second colour.

3. Keep this going for as many rows as you need. Keep whichever yarn is being carried up the edge smooth by gently pulling it. You want it to reach up without getting baggy but not be so tight that it pulls the edge of your knitting down.

Slipped stitch patterns

You can combine knit and purl stitches in almost infinite ways to make different textures of knitting. We've covered the difference between garter, stocking and ribbed stitches (see page 46–8), but some of the patterns in this book introduce you to more intricate stitch patterns. Even the most simple stitches are the building blocks of intricate lacework.

SLIPPED STITCHES

The Hot Water Bottle Cover on page 140 makes use of a very simple stitch pattern to create a cozy texture with an almost woven appearance. It's made by slipping stitches from the left to right needle without knitting them.

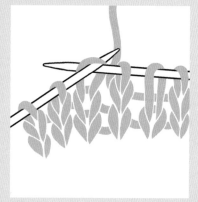
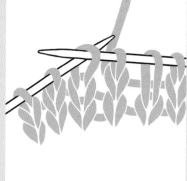
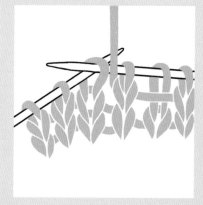

1.
There are two different ways to slip a stitch – knitwise and purlwise. Knitwise means by putting your right needle into the stitch as though you were going to knit it.

2.
…and purlwise means as though you were going to purl it.

3.
To create the woven appearance, slip the stitches purlwise. Move the yarn to the front of your work – as though you were going to purl – and then slip your stitch (without knitting it). Move the yarn to the back and knit the next stitch. You'll be able to see the yarn in front of the slipped stitch as a bar of yarn. Purl the next row – the slipped stitches will pull up to the next row.

Holding yarn double

Holding yarn double is a great way to add colour and texture to your work. This technique works particularly well with light and fluffy yarns such as mohair, and it is used in the Slouchy Beanie on page 136. There isn't much more to it than finding the ends of both yarns you want to work with, lining them up and starting to cast. The yarns quickly start to act as if they were always meant to be knitted together. If you think you'll get in a tangle, you can wind your two yarns together before you start knitting.

Adding mohair to, for example, a merino yarn not only adds a soft fuzz but also means you can play with the colour of your finished project. You can use a matching mohair to blend in perfectly with the colour of the merino, or use a contrast colour to add an extra dimension to the original colour.

You don't just have to use mohair when knitting with doubled yarn. If you've got a pattern that calls for double knitting weight (DK) yarn and you've found the perfect yarn but it's a 4-ply weight, you can hold two strands of the 4-ply together to create an 8-ply DK weight. You can either use two balls held together, or knit from both ends of the same ball of yarn – you'll need to reach into the middle and pull out one end from the very centre of the ball. You can then hold this with the yarn end from the outside and your yarn will double up perfectly.

Troubleshooting

Even the most experienced knitters make mistakes. Being able to understand and fix what's happened is the key to confident knitting. Knitting can always be undone – there's almost nothing you can't fix.

COUNTING YOUR ROWS

Some patterns require you to work a specific number of rows – and if you don't keep track as you go, it can be daunting to try to work out how far you've got. Remember, you can pop a row counter on your needles at the start of your work to keep track. There are also various tricks to help you count your rows.

Columns

Although we think of knitting being in horizontal rows, you can also think about your individual stitches being in columns, with each stitch being on top of its corresponding stitch in the row below.

Pick a column of stitches in the middle of your work and count the number of stitches in that column. The cast-on row doesn't count, so don't include it in your total – but remember to include the row that's on your needles.

This is a lot easier in stocking stitch because you can clearly see the 'V' shape of each stitch. The smoother fabric makes it easy to see the grid of stitches and rows.

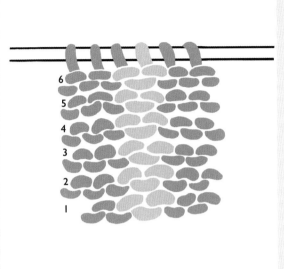 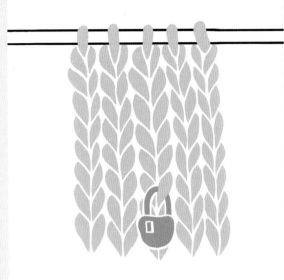

Ridges

Although individual stitches aren't as clear in garter stitch, you can see horizontal ridges across your work.

Each ridge (numbered in the illustration above) represents two rows, so count the number of ridges and multiply this by two. If you've knitted an odd number of rows, you'll have an incomplete-looking ridge below your needle, so this only counts as half a ridge before you multiply by two.

If you're not sure whether you've got an odd or an even number of rows, you can use the tail from your cast on to make sure (if you used the knitting-on method to cast on). If the working yarn is on the same side as your tail, you've knitted an odd number of rows; if the working yarn is on the other side of your work to the tail, you've knitted an even number of rows.

Stitch markers

If you have a lot of rows to count, clipping a locking stitch marker or safety pin every ten rows can make it easier to keep track. The same goes if you have a lot of stitches to count – slipping a marker on your needles every ten stitches makes it much easier to count.

PUTTING STITCHES THE RIGHT WAY ROUND

Sometimes you'll encounter a stitch that just doesn't seem to sit right on your needles. This is usually because it has become twisted. This is a really useful thing to know how to fix if you ever have to undo several rows and you need to put a lot of stitches back on a needle – you can make sure they all sit on your needle the right way round.

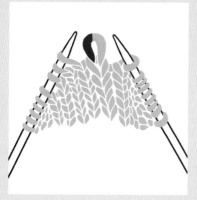

1.
When your stitch isn't on a needle, it's easier to see that it is really a loop of yarn coming out of the stitch below it. The loop has two sides or 'legs' – a left leg (coloured in grey, above) and a right leg.

2a. <u>Correct</u>
The illustration above shows where the right leg of the stitch should be – it should be in front when it is on the needle.

2b. <u>Incorrect</u>
If the left leg is in front, it will be harder to knit into and it will twist when you knit into it, leading to uneven knitting.

To set a twisted stitch straight, put the right needle into the back leg of the stitch and slip it off the left needle. You can now use the left needle to pick up the left leg of the stitch from front to back, reorienting the stitch the right way round.

PICKING UP DROPPED STITCHES

It's likely that the most frequent mistake you'll make is dropping stitches. This happens when a stitch falls off your left needle without moving on to the right needle. It can seem disastrous, but you can save yourself from undoing all your work by picking up the stitch.

 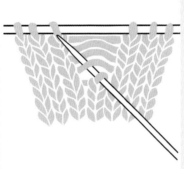 

1.
You can identify a dropped stitch by a 'ladder' running down between two stitches on your needle. Spread your knitting out so you can see the 'rungs' of this laddered stitch and put a spare needle into the stitch so that it doesn't ladder further.

2.
Now put the point of that needle under the 'rung' just above the stitch and pull your dropped stitch over it. Pull the 'rung' through the stitch to make a new loop – that brings the dropped stitch up one row.

3.
Repeat until you have no more rungs above your dropped stitch; you can now slip it on to your working needle. You can also use a crochet hook instead of a spare needle to hook the rungs through your dropped stitch.

EXTRA STITCHES

Sometimes you'll find that your work is growing wider as well as longer without you meaning it to. When you first start knitting, it's easy to add extra stitches that make your work too wide or even to add holes. It's hard to correct these without ripping out (undoing your work) and starting again, but you can at least identify what you might be doing wrong – and try not to do it again.

Splitting a stitch

Sometimes you can split the yarn in a stitch and accidentally knit the same stitch twice. Make sure you're putting your right needle into the whole stitch when you come to knit it and you aren't just picking up a few of the strands from it.

Extra yarn over needles

If you have extra stitches in your work and little round holes that aren't part of the pattern, you've been adding extra yarn over needles (see page 38) and knitting them as normal stitches in the next row.

These can form in a couple of different ways:

1. When making a new stitch, you wrap the yarn around your right needle but don't pull it through the stitch properly. On the next row, you'll still have that yarn wrapped on the needle and the stitch from the row below. If you knit both of these, you'll have added a stitch. If you spot this on the row after you do it, you can pull the wrapped yarn through the stitch it was meant to go through and fix it.

2. If you're working a pattern with knits and purls, check you're not wrapping the yarn around the right needle when you move it from back to front – otherwise you'll end up with extra yarn over needles.

Knitting your first stitch twice

When you reach the end of a knit row and turn your work, your yarn will be at the front of your knitting. Before you knit another row, move the yarn to the back under the left needle. If you miss this step, the yarn will pull the stitch up and over your left needle and it will be really easy to accidentally knit into both legs of the stitch.

In projects where the edge is left visible, such as in scarves, you can slip the first stitch of each row. This gives your work a neat edge (and ensures that you won't accidentally knit the first stitch twice!).

Undoing your work

Sometimes there's nothing for it but to undo your work. Frustrating though it is, it can be better to undo a few rows than to plough ahead and have to undo a lot more – an (undone) stitch in time saves nine! There are two different methods of undoing your work: ripping out and tinking.

RIPPING OUT

Ripping out your knitting is the quickest and most dramatic method of undoing multiple rows of work. It involves sliding your work off the needles and pulling on the working yarn so your knitting unravels. It can feel counterintuitive, but there are some ways you can make it a lot less scary.

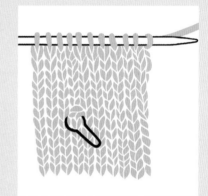

- Fixing your work isn't something you want to do in a rush. Take your time, and make sure you have plenty of space to work in and good lighting. This will make picking your stitches back up again so much easier.

- You don't want to rip out more than you need to. Once you've identified where you want to go back, pop a safety pin or a locking stitch marker just underneath it so that you know where to stop.

- If you're ripping out work with stitch markers in, take a note of where they were – or even a quick photo – so that you can put them back in the right place when you're done.

- Some yarns rip out more easily than others. Very drapey cottons will fall apart and you'll need to be careful that you don't lose extra stitches. Fluffy yarns such as mohair really grip together, so need some help unravelling.

- Ripping out is sometimes referred to as 'frogging' because 'rip it' sounds a bit like a frog going 'ribbit ribbit'. So, if you hear someone saying they 'frogged an entire project', then you know they ripped out the whole thing.

Using a lifeline
If you don't feel confident picking up all of the stitches again, you can put in a 'lifeline' of spare yarn that will hold a row safe for you.

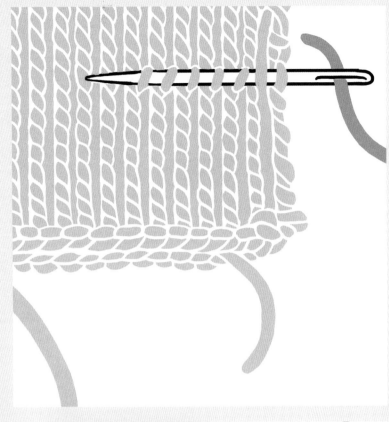

1.
Thread a darning needle with some spare yarn and, in the row before your mistake, pick up each stitch onto the needle. Working from right to left, pick up the right leg of each 'V'-shaped stitch.

2.
Work all the way along the row, then pull the spare yarn through so that it runs all the way through the row. When you rip out your working yarn, it will stop at this row because the stitches are held safely on the scrap yarn.

3.
When you're ready, slide the knitting needles out of your work and pull the working yarn away from it so that your stitches start unravelling. Wind the yarn back around the ball as you go, otherwise you'll end up with a big tangle.

TINKING

Undoing your work stitch by stitch is sometimes known as tinking, because 'tink' is 'knit' backwards – and you can think of this as reversing the knitting you have just done.

Rather than work from your left needle onto your right, here you'll be undoing the stitches on your right needle and putting them back on your left. This is useful if you only want to undo a few stitches or don't want to rip out your work if you think it will all fall apart.

Put your left needle into the stitch below the first stitch on your right needle, from front to back. Slip the stitch off your right needle and pull the yarn out. This method works exactly the same for purl (although is not referred to as lruping!).

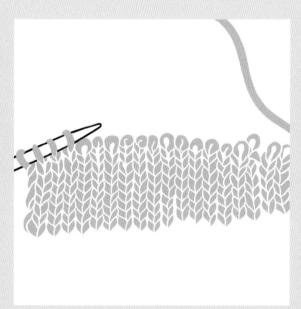

Putting your stitches back on the needle

When you're done ripping out, you need to get your live stitches back onto a needle. It can be helpful to use a smaller size of needle to pick them up initially, as it will be easier to get it through the loops of your stitches. You can then slip your stitches from this smaller needle to one of the correct size – and if any are twisted, you can untwist them when you do so.

If you are putting the stitches onto a smaller needle first, start at the working yarn end. Then when you slip the stitches back onto the correct needle, the working yarn will be at the pointed end of the needle. Otherwise, start at the non-working-yarn side so that the working yarn is at the pointed end of your needle when you're done.

Count your stitches to make sure you haven't dropped any and pick up any slightly laddered ones.

Tension

The tension of your knitting refers to how tightly or loosely you are knitting. If your tension is too tight, your knitting will be very dense and your stitches difficult to work. If your tension is too loose, your knitting will be floppy and slip off your needles. A nice even tension comes with practise, but you can make adjustments if you're struggling:

- New knitters often knit very tightly because they yank their yarn as they make each stitch. Remember, you're not knotting each stitch – just gently pulling it into place.

- If your stitches look uneven when your project is finished, give your knitting a gentle stretch first horizontally and then vertically. Your stitches will move into a more even tension.

- You may find a pattern that asks you to knit a swatch to test your tension (it's sometimes called a gauge square). You can use it to check that your tension matches what the pattern is indicating. It saves you discovering half way through a jumper that it's not going to fit! You should knit this 10cm (4in) square before you start the project properly. The pattern will tell you how many stitches to cast on and how many rows to work in a particular needle size. If it ends up smaller than 10cm (4in) square, switch to bigger needles; if it comes out larger, switch to smaller needles.

Finishing your work

The finishing touches are often integral to the outcome of your project. It can seem daunting to sew your pieces together when you've spent so much time on the actual knitting, but a bit of patience can really make your project look its best.

   The key to sewing your knitting together is consistency. It doesn't matter which method of sewing you choose, as long as you keep doing the same thing all the way around. This ensures that your knitting looks neat and regular.

WHIP STITCH

Whip stitches work well for sewing together a seam that you don't mind being slightly visible, or sewing together two cast-off edges – for a cushion cover, perhaps.

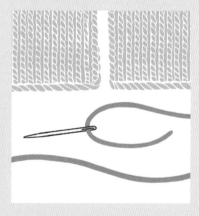

1.
When you cut the yarn at the end of your project, leave a long tail that you can use to sew your pieces together. Thread the yarn onto a blunt tapestry needle.

2.
Hold the two pieces of knitting that you're joining with wrong sides together and line up the edges you're going to sew.

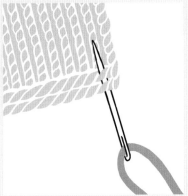

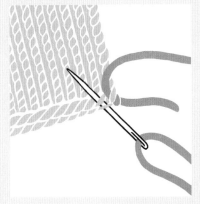

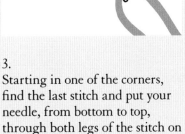

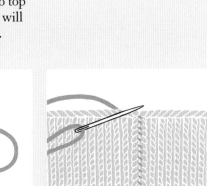

3.
Starting in one of the corners, find the last stitch and put your needle, from bottom to top, through both legs of the stitch on both pieces of knitting.

4.
Pull the yarn through, then repeat this for the next stitch along, going from bottom to top through both stitches. This will create your first whip stitch.

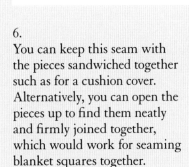

5.
Keep working along the two pieces, always stitching from bottom to top to keep it neat.

6.
You can keep this seam with the pieces sandwiched together such as for a cushion cover. Alternatively, you can open the pieces up to find them neatly and firmly joined together, which would work for seaming blanket squares together.

MATTRESS STITCH

To join two pieces of stocking stitch together, you can use a technique called mattress stitch. This works better with a separate piece of yarn and not the tail from your cast-on or cast-off edge.

2.
Mattress stitch works by sewing together the horizontal 'bars' of yarn that run between the 'Vs' of your stitches. Gently pull your knitting horizontally and you'll see the bars between the stitches.

1.
Lay your finished pieces next to each other, right side up, with the stitches going the same way.

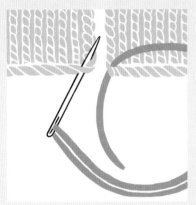 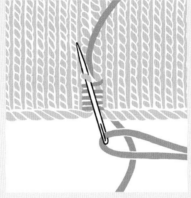 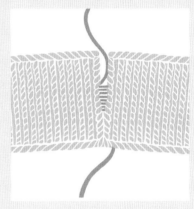

3.
Thread a blunt sewing or tapestry needle and bring it up through the bottom corner stitch of one of your pieces, leaving a tail. Take your needle under the bar between the first two stitches on the other piece of knitting.

4.
This technique creates a seam, so only work one stitch from the edge – otherwise you'll lose a large portion of your work inside the seam. Move back to the first side and take your needle under the bar on the row above the one where you first started sewing.

Continue working vertically up your work, alternating from one side to the other and sewing under the bars, until you have joined the whole seam.

5.
Gently pull on both ends of your yarn – your sewing will disappear as the stitching tightens. If you're struggling to keep the pieces lined up while you sew them together, pin them together with safety pins before you start.

CLOSING UP HATS

When you finish a hat, don't cast off the last few stitches. Instead, thread your yarn back through the live stitches and pull it tight.

 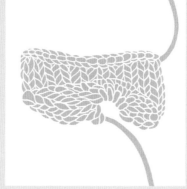

1.
Cut your working yarn – it should be as long as the width of your knitting plus roughly the length of your forearm. Thread this yarn onto a blunt sewing needle.

   If you're knitting flat (rather than in the round), take the sewing needle to the last stitch on your knitting needle – the one furthest away from your most recent stitch. When you sew your hat together, these two stitches will be next to each other. Thread the sewing needle through the stitch purlwise.

2.
Keep working along the stitches, threading your needle through them from left to right. Slide your knitting off the needle and pull the stitches tight.

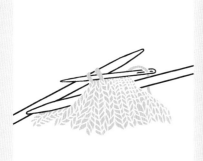

3.
If you knitted your hat in the round, you thread your sewing needle through the next stitch on your left-hand needle, as your hat is already joined together as a tubular piece and all you're doing is closing the gap at the top.

WEAVING IN ENDS

There are lots of different ways to weave the ends of your yarn into your projects. There is no one magic technique, but here are some pointers.

- Make sure you leave your yarn ends long enough to weave in easily once they are threaded on a needle – a good 15cm (6in) will be the right length.

- If your work has an inside and an outside, make sure that the cut end of your yarn is on the inside, so that it isn't visible.

- You don't need to knot your yarn, because the weaving will hold it in place.

- Sew with a blunt tapestry needle – it'll go into the stitches easily without splitting the yarn. Tapestry needles also have nice big eyes for threading yarn.

- Don't sew the yarn end in so tightly that it pulls your knitting out of shape. Try to keep the same tension as your knitting.

- Remember to weave up and down and not just in a straight line – otherwise the yarn end can be easily pulled out.

Ideally you want to camouflage your sewn-in tail as much as possible, which you can do by weaving it along the stitches of one row.

- Thread the leftover yarn tail onto your tapestry needle.

- Looking at the wrong side of your work, identify the row just above the tail. You can follow the yarn in this row as it winds up into the stitches above it and down into the stitches below.

- Still working just on this side of your knitting, follow this line with your needle, mimicking the original stitches – see the grey yarn in the illustration. Sew along this line for 3–5cm (1–2in), then cut the yarn tail.

POMPOMS

You can give a stylish finishing touch to a hat by adding a pompom in a contrasting colour. It can also hide any messy sewing together on the top! You can buy pompom makers that make the process a bit easier, but you can also go the old-school route and use a sturdy bit of cardboard. They both make pompoms in exactly the same manner.

Make sure you leave a long tail on the pompom, as you will need this to sew the pompom on to the top of a hat or the corners of a scarf.

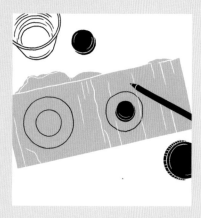 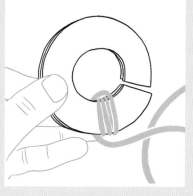 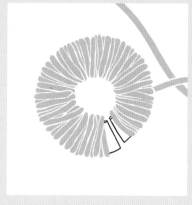

1.
Cut out a circle out of cardboard – the size of your circle determines the size of your pompom. You can use a mug or a glass to draw around. Draw a smaller circle within the big one to create a doughnut shape.

2.
Snip into the middle of the circle, then cut the smaller circle out – you'll end up with a doughnut-shaped piece of card. Trace round this onto a second piece of card so that you have two matching pieces.

Hold these two pieces together and start winding your yarn around them. You can use the gap where you sliced into your circles to get the yarn round easily.

3.
Keep wrapping until your circles are full. You want the centre circle to be almost completely full for a big fluffy pompom. Don't worry if you don't fill right to the edges of where you cut into the middle – your pompom will fluff up and hide that gap. Cut your working yarn, leaving a long tail.

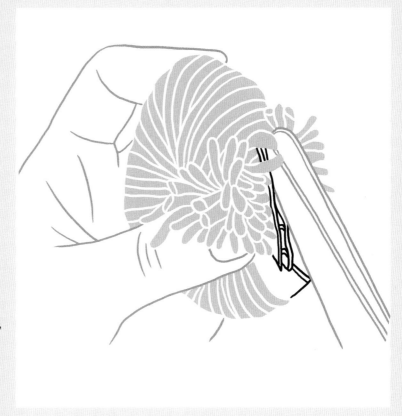

4.
Holding on tightly to the middle, put the point of your scissors between the two cardboard rings and start snipping the yarn. Sharp scissors with a small point are useful here.

5.
When you've worked your way around the pompom, slide a length of yarn between the two cardboard rings and tie it tightly. Wrap the ends back around and tie a double knot – you want to get the knot as close to the centre of the pompom as possible.

6.
Remove the pieces of cardboard and, holding onto the tail, give your pompom a good shake. That will help fluff it up and show you any pieces that need a trim. The trick to a perfect pompom is to give it a haircut afterwards.

TASSELS

Tassels are really versatile additions to your knitting – they can be added to scarves or hung off bags or even popped on a keyring to stand on their own. They're simple to make – all you need is some yarn and cardboard.

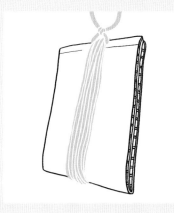

1.
Cut a rectangle of cardboard the same length as your desired tassel. Wrap the yarn around the cardboard until it's as full as you want your tassel to be.

2.
Slide another length of yarn under the wrapped yarn and up to the top of the piece of cardboard. Tie it tightly around the yarn at the top.

3.
Cut the wrapped yarn at the other end of the tassel and remove the cardboard.

4.
Take another length of yarn and thread it through a tapestry needle. About 2.5cm (1in) from the top, start to wrap the loose end of the yarn around the tassel as tightly as you can.

5.
Keep wrapping the yarn around the tassel until you're happy with the width.

6.
Thread the needle underneath the wrapped yarn and pull it through at the top of the tassel to help bind the wrapped yarn in place. Trim the ends of the tassel to neaten them up.

Caring for your handknits

Once you've finished knitting your items, you'll want to take good care of them. You don't want all that effort to go to waste because you threw a coffee-stained scarf in the washing machine and shrank it!

Washing

Keep the paper band that came around your yarn – it will give you the washing instructions. Here are some general tips on keeping your knits clean without ruining them:

- Some wools will shrink or felt (get really tight and dense) if they're washed at too high a temperature. These need to be hand washed in cool water with gentle detergent. You can get wool-specific detergents – some of these don't even need to be rinsed out.

- Others wools are 'superwash' and can go in a normal warm cycle – they've been processed in a way that helps them survive a cool wash. Cotton yarns can go in the washing machine on a gentle setting. Acrylic items can be washed with your normal load.

- If you're washing something that will hold a lot of water, once you've rinsed it through, lay it flat on a towel, roll it up like a sausage and stand on it. The water moves from the knitted item to the towel, which is easier to dry than a big yarn blanket.

- To dry your knitwear, pull it back into shape gently and dry it flat.

Moths

Clothes moths will eat any yarns made of protein – sheep's wool, alpaca, mohair and so on. There are a few things you can do to keep them from ruining all your good work.

- Keep your knitwear and your yarn stash in a sealed container so that moths can't get in.

- If you're handwashing any knitted items, pop a couple of drops of lavender oil in the water – moths dislike the scent.

- Moths won't eat cotton or acrylic yarns, so if you're worried about your projects being munched away, stick to those fibres.

Projects

Chunky scarf

It's something of a knitting tradition to start with a scarf, and this super chunky one, knitted on 12mm (US 17) needles, is as close as knitting gets to instant gratification! Go super bright for a pop of colour or snuggle down in a gentle pastel cloud.

YOU WILL NEED

Rowan Big Wool (or other super chunky yarn):
3 x 100g (80m/87yd) balls in 78 Yoke
12mm (US 17) knitting needles
Tapestry needle

SIZE

Approx. 21 x 172cm (8 x 68in)

Cast on 24 stitches.

This cast-on edge determines the width of the scarf, so you can cast on more or fewer stitches if you'd like a wider or a skinnier scarf – just be sure to cast on a multiple of four stitches so that the 2 by 2 rib lines up.

Row 1: [k2, p2] to end of row.

This makes the first row of your ribbed scarf, alternating two knit stitches with two purl stitches. When moving your yarn from the back of your work to the front (and vice versa), remember not to wrap it around your needles: that would create an extra stitch and throw everything out.

Row 2: [k2, p2] to end of row.

Because you're working a number of stitches that divides into four (for the four stitches of your k2, p2 pattern), each row is the same in the scarf, making it easy to follow. If you added an extra two stitches at the end, you'd have to make sure you p2, k2 on every other row – otherwise your ribs wouldn't line up. There isn't a right or a wrong side with this project, as both sides end up the same.

Repeat this row until you get to the end of a row and are nearly out of yarn – but have at least a metre left.

Your scarf can be as long or as short as you like; you just need to make sure you have enough yarn left to cast off with.

Project continues overleaf

PROJECTS

Cast off in [k2, p2] rib.

Cast off by knitting your first two stitches and passing the first over the second. Then, because you're still following your k2, p2 pattern, purl the next stitch and pass the previous stitch over it. Keep working along your left-hand needle, alternating 2 knit stitches and 2 purl, until you have one stitch left. Pull the tail of your yarn through this stitch tightly to secure it.

Finishing your scarf

Thread the loose end of your yarn through a large-eyed needle. Weave the yarn back through your knitting, following a line of stitches so that it disappears into your work (see page 80). Repeat for the yarn hanging from your cast-on edge.

TO MAKE A BLANKET

This scarf is perfect for converting into a super-cozy blanket. Use the exact same k2, p2 rib pattern, but cast on 60 stitches instead. You'll need a lot more wool, too – about 600m/650yd – and you might find it easier to fit your stitches on a long circular needle than on straight needles. That way you're not bunching all your work up to fit on a single 30cm (12in) needle.

Reusable face wipes

If you're trying to reduce your waste, reusable face wipes and cotton rounds are a great way to stop your bathroom bin overflowing. Use 100% natural fibre yarns such as cotton or linen and they can be composted at the end of their lives. The stocking stitch centre of this facecloth gives you a smooth side for wiping away make-up and a textured side for really getting clean.

YOU WILL NEED

Erika Knight Gossypium Cotton
(or other DK yarn):
1 x 50g (100m/109yd) ball in
500 Milk
4mm (US 6) knitting needles
Tapestry needle

SIZE

Approx. 15 x 15cm (6 x 6in)

Cast on 44 stitches.
The size of your facecloth doesn't need to be precise, but this will make one that's approximately 15cm (6in) square.

Rows 1–4: k.
Knitting these four plain rows creates a garter stitch border without which your facecloth would roll into a little tube.

Row 5: k.

Row 6: k4, p36, k4.
Rows 5 and 6 create the body of your facecloth – it's mainly stocking stitch with a garter stitch border so the cloth keeps its shape. A knit row followed by another knit row is garter stitch. A knit row followed by a purl row is stocking stitch.

Repeat rows 5 and 6 25 times (56 rows in total).
If you're not sure which row you should knit next, look at the fabric facing you from the left-hand needle. Lots of flat Vs mean that you're working a right-side row and should repeat row 5. Lots of little bumps mean that you're working a wrong-side row and should repeat row 6. You may also find a row counter useful, as it saves you counting all those rows.

Rows 57–60: k.
This completes your garter stitch border. Cast off and weave in loose ends (see page 80).

Project continues overleaf

TO MAKE A MINI CLOTH

This miniature version is good for taking off eye make-up. It's exactly the same design, just on a smaller scale – roughly 4 x 5cm (1½ x 2 in).

Cast on 11 stitches.

Rows 1–2: k.

Row 3: k.

Row 4: k2, p7, k2.

Repeat rows 3 and 4 four times (12 rows in total).

Rows 13–14: k.

Cast off and weave in loose ends (see page 80).

REUSABLE FACE WIPES

Colourblock cushion cover

This statement cushion is simple to make but has a big impact. It uses super chunky yarn, so it doesn't take long to whip up both sides, plus it has a really clear stitch definition to show off your knitting skills. Play with colours and liven up your sofa!

YOU WILL NEED

Wool and the Gang Crazy Sexy Wool (or other super chunky yarn):
  1 x 200g ball (80m/87yd) in 186 Pink Sherbert
  1 x 200g ball (80m/87yd) in 083 Sherpa Blue
10mm (US 15) knitting needles
Measuring tape
Tapestry needle
40 x 40cm (16 x 16in) cushion pad

SIZE

Approx. 40 x 40cm (16 x 16in)

Cast on 34 stitches in Pink Sherbert.
The beauty of this super chunky yarn is that it takes very few stitches to make a cushion cover.

Row 1: k.

Row 2: p.
This cushion is knitted in stocking stitch, but don't worry about it rolling up while you knit – once it's sewn up with a cushion pad inside, it will keep a flat shape.

Repeat rows 1 and 2 until your work measures 27cm (11in).
With this super chunky yarn, it won't take very long! At the start of the next row, cut your first yarn and change to Sherpa Blue. You need to leave a long enough tail of both your yarns to be able to weave each one in later.

Continue repeating rows 1 and 2 for another 13cm (4½in) or until your work measures 40cm (16in) in total, ending on a purl row.

Cast off knitwise.

Repeat the instructions to make the back of the cushion.
Now repeat this for the back of the cushion, reversing your colours: cast on with Sherpa Blue and switch to Pink Sherbert. Not only does having the two different sides make for a more interesting cushion, it's also a more efficient use of your yarn as it uses the same amount of both colours. You'll now have two squares of knitted fabric.

Project continues overleaf

Finishing your cushion

Put your work wrong sides together – you'll want to line up your stitches so they go in the same direction on both sides. Sewing from the right side of your knitting, work along three sides of the cushion. Insert your cushion pad and then sew up the final side of the cushion. This yarn isn't twisted, so it can pull apart easily. Cut a new length of yarn for each side of the cushion so that it doesn't get pulled too much.

Remember, the best tip for sewing up is consistency! It doesn't matter which technique you use, whether you use mattress stitch (see page 76) or whip stitch (see page 74) or just a running stitch; if you use the same stitch all the way round, it'll look neat!

Mug cozy

A cozy way to keep your hands safe from hot drinks! It's worked in moss stitch – a chequerboard texture that looks like a lot more work than it is. Simple and super-fast to make, this makes a great gift.

YOU WILL NEED

Drops Karisma (or other DK yarn):
  1 x 50g ball (100m/110yd) in
  11 Orange
4mm (US 6) knitting needles
Tapestry needle

SIZE

Approx. 14 x 6cm (5½ x 2½in)

Cast on 50 stitches.

If your favourite mug is an unusual size you can adjust the number of stitches, but you need to make sure you have an even number – otherwise you'll end up knitting a plain old rib!

Row 1: [k1, p1] to end of row.

Row 2: [p1, k1] to end of row.

The first row of this pattern is like a normal 1 x 1 rib, but on the second (wrong-side) row, you're working the opposite stitch. This creates a chequerboard texture – you'll know you've gone awry if your stitches start lining up in columns rather than in a grid.

Repeat these 2 rows 7 more times (16 rows in total).

You can, of course, adjust this pattern to fit taller or shorter mugs.

Cast off in [k1, p1] pattern.

If you cast the entire cozy off knitwise, you'd have a very obvious 'rope' of cast-off stitches along the top. By continuing to work your stitches in k1, p1 – before slipping the previous stitch over to cast off – your cast-off row disappears in with the rest of the pattern.

Sew up the short sides and weave in ends.

Finishing your mug cozy

This cozy is designed for a mug without a handle. If you want to dress up a mug with a handle, just sew up the top and bottom two rows, leaving a gap to put the handle through.

Chunky hat with pompom

This hat is designed to go with the Chunky Scarf (see page 90). It's knitted flat and sewn up afterwards, so it's a great second project to practise a few more techniques. And you can add a bright pompom to cheer up any grey days.

(see page 90)

YOU WILL NEED

Rowan Big Wool (or other super chunky yarn):
  1 x 100g (80m/87yd) ball in 056 Glum
12mm (US 17) knitting needles
Tapestry needle
Optional: Super chunky yarn for pompom

SIZE

Approx. 28 x 17cm (11 x 6½in), without the pompom

Cast on 40 stitches.
This cast-on edge determines the circumference of your hat, so you can adjust it for a tighter or looser fit. If you do adjust the number of stitches, do so in multiples of 4.

Row 1: [k2, p2] to end of row.
This hat is knitted almost exactly like its matching scarf. Working in a ribbed stitch means that your hat has enough stretch to stay on your head.

Row 2: [k2, p2] to end of row.
This hat is knitted flat and then sewn up so turn your work at the end of each row and continue working the ribbed stitches.

Repeat rows 1 and 2 until hat measures 30cm (12in) long.
We've knitted this hat with a generous folded brim to keep it super cozy. If you don't want a brimmed hat, you can knit fewer rows before starting the decreasing – you can stop after 20cm (9in).

Next row: [k2tog, p2] to end of row.
This row starts the decreases that makes your hat smaller at the crown than at the brim. You're still following a repeated pattern, but on this row you'll knit two stitches together before purling two stitches. This reduces your stitch count by 10, leaving you with 30 stitches.

Next row: [k2tog, p1] to end of row.
Continue decreasing on the next row. You've only got three stitches per repeat on this row, so you only need to purl one stitch before the next knit two together. You should have 20 stitches at the end of this row.

Project continues overleaf

PROJECTS

Next row: [k2tog] to end of row.

On this row, there are no purl stitches – knit two stitches together ten times for your final set of decreases, after which you'll have ten stitches left on your needles.

Finishing your hat

Rather than cast off these ten stitches, you're going to thread the yarn back through them and pull them tight. To do this, you will need to cut your yarn, leaving a long enough tail to sew up the side of the hat, and thread it onto a yarn needle.

Thread the needle through the stitch at the other end of your knitting needle to your working yarn and continue, making sure you thread through each stitch, until you get back to the last stitch you knitted. Slide the stitches off your knitting needle and pull tight.

Sew up side of hat: Still using the long tail of yarn you've pulled tight, work down the side of the hat, sewing the two sides together (see page 78) and matching each row of knitting to keep your seam even. When you reach the cast-on edge, weave the tail and the cast-on tail into the inside of the hat (which might be the outside if you are going to turn up the brim.)

Make pompom and sew onto hat: If you want to really make this hat stand out, attach a pompom to the top. Make a pompom (see page 82), leaving a long tail. Sew it to the crown, then pass the tail back through the middle of the pompom several times; this stops it from wobbling and keeps it securely attached.

TO MAKE A HEADBAND

If you'd rather not have an enclosed hat, cast off your knitting after 12cm (4¾in), remembering to cast off still following the k2, p2 rib. The final size will be roughly 20 x 10cm (8 x 4in). Sew up the side seam and you have a headband to keep your ears warm and your ponytail high.

Doorstop

This big and bold doorstop uses colour blocking for maximum impact. Your newfound knitting skills will open doors for you – literally!

YOU WILL NEED

Drops Paris (or other
  Aran weight yarn):
  3 x 50g (75m/82yd) balls in
  01 Apricot
  2 x 50g (75m/82yd) balls in
  23 Light Grey
4.5mm (US 7) knitting needles
Tapestry needle
2kg (4½lb) dried split peas
Toy stuffing

SIZE

Approx. 23 x 25cm (9 x 10in)

Cast on 10 stitches, leaving a long tail to sew up with later.

Row 1: p.

Row 2: [k1, m1] 9 times, k1.
This is the bottom of the door stop: this and subsequent increase rows create its base. Remember m1 means 'make 1 stitch' – see page 39 for more information.

Row 3 and all wrong-side rows: p.
This instruction tells you to purl every other row – odd-numbered rows will now be omitted from the pattern, because you know to purl them.

Row 4: [k2, m1] 9 times, k1.

Row 6: [k3, m1] 9 times, k1.

Row 8: [k4, m1] 9 times, k1.

Row 10: [k5, m1] 9 times, k1.

Row 12: [k6, m1] 9 times, k1.

Row 14: [k7, m1] 9 times, k1.

Row 16: [k8, m1] 9 times, k1.

Row 18: [k9, m1] 9 times, k1.

Row 20: [k10, m1] 9 times, k1.

Row 22: [k11, m1] 9 times, k1.

Row 24: [k12, m1] 9 times, k1.

Project continues overleaf

PROJECTS

Rows 25–41: Work 17 rows in stocking stitch, starting with a purl row.

Row 42: [k11, k2tog] 9 times, k1.
Adding a few decrease rows before the top of the doorstop gives it more shaping.

Rows 43–59: Work 17 rows in stocking stitch, starting with a purl row.

Row 60: [k10, k2tog] 9 times, k1.

Rows 61–77: Change yarn to Light Grey. Work 17 rows in stocking stitch, starting with a purl row.

Row 78: [k9, k2tog] 9 times, k1.
As at the beginning, the alternate purl rows aren't included in the pattern – just remember to work them!

Row 80: [k8, k2tog] 9 times, k1.

Row 82: [k7, k2tog] 9 times, k1.

Row 84: [k6, k2tog] 9 times, k1.

Row 86: [k5, k2tog] 9 times, k1.

Row 88: [k4, k2tog] 9 times, k1.

Row 90: [k3, k2tog] 9 times, k1.

Row 92: [k2, k2tog] 9 times, k1.

Row 94: [k1, k2tog] 9 times, k1.

Row 96: [k2tog] 9 times, k1.

Finishing your doorstop

Do not cast off; instead, cut the yarn and thread it through the remaining stitches, but don't pull tight yet. Next, thread the yarn tail from the cast-on stitches through a tapestry needle and, starting from the bottom, sew up the sides until you reach the final decrease section. Fill the doorstop with dried split peas – this will make it heavy enough to hold your door open. Continue sewing up and fill the remaining space with toy stuffing. Thread the yarn tail through the cast-off stitches, slide the knitting off the needle and pull your final stitches tight. Weave in both ends securely.

Tablet case

Keep your screens unscratched with this simple but colourful tablet case. It's designed for a 25cm (10in) tablet, but you can easily customize it to fit a device of your choosing by casting on more or fewer stitches.

YOU WILL NEED
Cascade 128 Superwash
   (or other chunky yarn):
   1 x 100g (117m/128yd) ball
   in 309 Granite Green
   1 x 100g (117m/128yd) ball
   in 307 Bright Cobalt
6mm (US 10) knitting needles
Tapestry needle

SIZE
Approx. 10 x 28cm (4 x 11in)

Cast on 26 stitches in Granite Green.
Because this tablet case is knitted in rib, it concertinas in on itself when the tablet isn't in it. Don't be alarmed! It has plenty of stretch.

Row 1: [k2, p2] to end of row.

Row 2: [p2, k2] to end of row.
This pattern isn't the same on each row as the number of stitches doesn't divide into four (for a 2 x 2 rib), so you need to check whether you're working the right side, which starts with a knit, or the wrong side, which starts with a purl.

    These two rows form the entire pattern. Keep working, alternating these rows and changing the colours as follows (the cast-on edge doesn't count as one of the rows):

Granite Green for 6 rows.

Bright Cobalt for 12 rows.

Granite Green for 6 rows.

Bright Cobalt for 12 rows.

Granite Green for 6 rows.

Bright Cobalt for 12 rows.

Granite Green for 12 rows.

Bright Cobalt for 6 rows.

Granite Green for 12 rows.

Project continues overleaf

Bright Cobalt for 6 rows.

Granite Green for 12 rows.

Bright Cobalt for 6 rows.

Cast off in rib.
That means cast off by knitting the first two stitches, then by purling two stitches, then knitting two, then purling two, to the end of the row.

<u>Finishing your tablet case</u>

Cut your yarn, leaving a long tail that you can sew up one side with.

Sew in all the yarn ends left over from your stripes, then fold your work in half so the short ends meet at the top and sew up both long sides.

TABLET CASE

Baby shoes

These adorable baby shoes make the perfect gift for new babies, whether they're worn or used to decorate a nursery. Made out of a simple T-shape, folded together, they're so quick and easy that you could even make them as an activity at a baby shower.

YOU WILL NEED

West Yorkshire Spinners Bo Peep
   Luxury Baby DK (or other
   DK yarn):
   1 x 50g (112m/122yd) ball in
   144 Sailboat
4mm (US 6) knitting needles
Tapestry needle
Optional: 2 buttons

Cast on 28 stitches.
This cast-on edge eventually becomes the top edge of the shoe. You can make a bigger shoe by casting on more stitches here.

Rows 1–12: k.

Row 13: Cast off 9 stitches, [k] to end of row.
You don't have to cast off a complete row – this technique is often used for adding shaping to pieces of garments, like the shoulders of sweaters. You'll be left with 19 stitches at the end of this row.

Row 14: Cast off 9 stitches, [k] to end of row.
You'll now have 9 stitches cast off on either side of your work and the central ten stitches remaining.

Rows 15–39: k.
These 24 rows form the sole of the baby shoe.

Finishing your baby shoes

Cast off, then cut the yarn leaving a long tail.
   With your knitting laid out like a capital T, fold both edges of the first 12 rows to line up with your cast-off edge. Sew these three layered edges together, then sew up each side of the sole.

Repeat for the second shoe.

If you like, you can sew a button to the top of the shoe – this will help hold the shoe in shape. Make sure you sew each button on very securely.

Wrist warmers

These cozy wrist warmers are a fun way of playing with colour and texture. Knitted in a wool and alpaca blend, they are soft and slightly fuzzy, perfect for peeking out of a sleeve on a cold winter's day.

If you struggle to knit these in the round, you can knit them flat and sew them up afterwards – for this, your alternate rows in Cobalt will always be purled and in Bottle will always be knitted.

YOU WILL NEED

Yarn Stories Fine Merino & Baby Alpaca DK (or other merino/ alpaca DK yarn):
  1 x 50g (120m/131yd) ball in 2503 Cobalt
  1 x 50g (120m/131yd) ball in 2501 Bottle
4 x 4mm (US 6) double-pointed needles

SIZE

Approx. 9 x 16½cm (3½ x 6½in)

Cast on 36 stitches in Cobalt and join in the round.

This pattern is a good opportunity to get comfortable with knitting small circumferences on double-pointed needles. It's easier to cast on onto one needle and then distribute your stitches across the other two – you'll have 12 stitches on each needle. Remember to pop a stitch marker in place so that you know where your rows start and end. Join in the round, checking that your stitches aren't twisted.

Row 1: [k1, p1] to end of round.

Row 2: k to end of round.

This mitt is designed in a broken rib stitch that alternates ribbed rows with plain rows. It creates an interesting texture with a little stretch. Your stitch marker will prompt you when you reach the end of the round (or row) and should therefore change the stitch.

Alternate these two rows for 10cm (4in), ending on a knit row.

Next row: [k1, p1] to end, turn work.

To create the thumb hole in this wrist warmer, a portion is knitted flat rather than in the round. When you reach the end of this row, rather than continuing in the round, turn your work as though you were knitting flat, with the stitch you just worked in your left hand. You can remove your stitch marker for this section.

Next row: [p] to end, turn work.

Alternate these two rows for 5cm (2in), ending on a purl row.

Keep working back and forth, continuing your broken rib, but worked flat. Remember, because you're now seeing the inside (or wrong side) of your wrist warmer, you need to purl those rows to keep the texture consistent.

Project continues overleaf

Cut the yarn, leaving a tail, and switch to your second colour.

It looks as if there should be some kind of trick or technique to changing colours but it really is as simple as working your next row in your new colour. Leave a long enough tail of both yarns to weave them in when you've finished.

Next row: [k] to end and join in the round again.

To close off the thumb hole and work the rest of the warmer, you need to join back in the round at the end of this row. Knit a row, then, without turning your work, knit into the first stitch of that row, closing the gap over the thumb hole. Remember to pop your stitch marker back in place.

Next row: [k] to end of round.

This section is knitted in garter stitch – but because you are working in the round, you have to alternate knit and purl rows.

Alternate these rows for 5cm (2in), working in the round, ending on a purl row.

<u>Finishing your wrist warmers</u>

Cast off knitwise and weave in ends. Casting off knitwise after a purl row looks more in keeping with the rest of the garter segment than if you cast off after a knit row.

Repeat for the second wrist warmer.

Angle scarf

This is not your average scarf. It plays with colour, shape and stitch patterns to make something really interesting – and let's not forget the tassels on the ends! The pattern is divided into three sections to make it easier to follow, and if you're struggling to visualise the shaping, imagine that laid out flat it makes a long, thin parallelogram.

YOU WILL NEED

Erika Knight Wild Wool (or
other Aran weight yarn):
 1 x 100g (170m/186yd) ball
 in 700 Amble
 1 x 100g (170m/186yd) ball
 in 709 Swagger
 1 x 100g (170m/186yd) ball
 in 703 Traipse
5.5mm (US 9) knitting needles
Tapestry needle

SIZE

Approx. 30 x 72cm (12 x 28½in)

SECTION ONE

Using Amble, cast on 5 stitches.

Next row: k.

Next row: k2, p1, k2.
This row sets up the main layout of the scarf – a stocking stitch centre with a two-stitch garter stitch border. If it helps you remember to knit only the two-stitch border, place stitch markers to show you where it starts and ends.

Row 1: k2, m1, k to end.
This row starts the shaping of the scarf. It increases on one side while remaining straight on the other side. The row count restarts here to show how the 20-row design works.

Row 2: k2, p2, k2.
Because you added a stitch in the previous row, there is now an extra stitch to purl.

Row 3: k2, m1, k to end.

Row 4: k2, p to last 2 stitches, k2.

Rows 5–16: repeat last 2 rows 6 times.
Patterns will often have instructions like this – don't panic! Just keep doing what the instructions tell you: here, you're adding a stitch on every knit row. By the end of Row 16, you'll have 13 stitches.

Project continues overleaf

Row 17: k2, m1, k to end.

Row 18: k.
This plain knit row adds some texture and definition before the eyelet row.

Row 19: k2, m1, [yon, k2tog] to last 2 stitches, k2.
Yes, knitting patterns sometimes look like algebra. The eyelets are made by a yarn over (yon) followed by a knit 2 together (k2tog). The decrease and increase cancel each other out, so you keep the same stitch count but create a hole in your work with the yarn over. The brackets bundle those two instructions together, so you repeat both of them until two stitches remain, both of which you knit.

Row 20: k.
You've now done your first repeat of the pattern – there are 17 stocking stitch rows with an increase on one side, followed by a three-row eyelet design. Repeat this 20-row pattern four more times. You add 10 stitches every repeat so, by the last repeat, you will have 55 stitches.

SECTION TWO

This section is worked with straight sides and no increases. It continues to use a 20-row repeat to create the eyelet design.

Change yarn to Swagger, cutting the first colour and leaving a long enough tail to sew in.

Row 1: k.

Row 2: k2, p51, k2.
Repeat these two rows seven more times.

Row 17: k.

Row 18: k.

Row 19: k3, [yon, k2tog] to last 2 stitches, k2.
Because there are an odd number of stitches in this section, you need to knit three stitches before you start the eyelet pattern.

Project continues overleaf

Row 20: k.

Repeat the whole of section two – this 20-row section you've just completed – three times. Then, in the same colour:

Next row: k.

Next row: k2, p51, k2.

Repeat these two rows seven more times (eight times in total).

SECTION THREE

The final section of the scarf changes colour again and begins to decrease on the opposite side to the increases. It starts with an eyelet row and then begins its own 20-row repeat.

Change yarn to Traipse, cutting the previous yarn.

Next row: k.

You switch the yarn colour a row before the eyelet section so that the colour change has a neat line – if you look at the back of your scarf, you'll see that the colours cross over each other.

Next row: k.

Next row: k2, [yon, k2tog] to last 5 stitches, yon, k3tog, k2.

The scarf begins decreasing at this point – the usual knit two together becomes a knit three together to combine both the eyelet pattern and the regular decreasing.

Next row: k.

After this eyelet section, you'll return to a 20-row repeat, as with the rest of the scarf.

Row 1: k to last 4 stitches, k2tog, k2.

Row 2: k2, p to last 2 stitches, k2.

Repeat these two rows eight more times (nine times in total).

Row 17: k to last 4 stitches, k2tog, k2.

Row 18: k.

Project continues overleaf

Row 19: k2, [yon, k2tog] to last 5 stitches, yon, k3tog, k2.

Row 20: k.

Repeat this section four times – it'll get quicker as you go along because of the decreases on the left side.

The final repeat doesn't have an eyelet row at the end.

Row 1: k to last 4 stitches, k2tog, k2.

Row 2: k2, p to last 2 stitches, k2.

Repeat these two rows eight more times (nine times in total).

Row 17: k to last 4 stitches, k2tog, k2.

Row 18: k.

Row 19: k to last 4 stitches, k2tog, k2.

Row 20: k.

Next row: cast off all stitches.

Finishing your scarf

Weave in the ends of your yarns and, using Swagger, make two tassels (see page 85). Sew one to each point of the scarf: you can use the tails from casting on and off to make them more secure.

ANGLE SCARF

Mitred square blanket

Mitred squares are a really effective way of knitting blanket squares without just working plain garter stitch. Your rows seem to fold in on themselves with a neat diagonal line across each square. The most satisfying thing about this blanket is that the rows get shorter as you work, so it seems to speed up towards the end.

YOU WILL NEED
Cascade 220 (or other
  Aran weight yarn):
  1 x 100g (200m/219yd) ball
  in 8021 Beige
  1 x 100g (200m/219yd) ball
  in 9683 Flax
  1 x 100g (200m/219yd) ball
  in 9682 Desert Flower
5.5mm (US 9) knitting needles
Stitch marker
Tapestry needle

SIZE
Approx. 60 x 80cm (24 x 32in)

Cast on 48 stitches in Beige.

Row 1: k24 stitches, place a marker, k24 stitches.
You'll find this stitch marker invaluable – otherwise you'll definitely find yourself knitting right on past where you're meant to decrease.

Row 2: k to 3 stitches before the marker, ssk, k1, slip marker, k1, k2tog, k to end of row.
This looks like a lot of instructions in one go, but take it one part at a time and you'll be fine. This row has two decreases in the centre, either side of your marker. Knit until three stitches before your marker, then do a slip, slip, knit (ssk). Knit a stitch, slip your marker and knit another stitch. These two stitches act as a buffer between your decreases to keep things neat. Knit two stitches together, then knit to the end of the row. You've decreased two stitches – now you'll have 46 stitches on your needle.

Row 3: k.
Every odd-numbered row in this blanket square is just plain knit stitch from now on.

Repeat rows 2 and 3 until only 2 stitches remain.
It's very satisfying to watch your rows get shorter and shorter as your decreases 'fold' into that central spine of the square.

Knit the last 2 stitches together. Cut your yarn, leaving a long tail.

This blanket uses two squares in Flax, four in Beige and six in Desert Flower. Each square is knitted separately and then they are sewn together.

Project continues overleaf

Finishing your blanket

To sew your blanket together, lay your finished squares out in the design you want, then thread your needle with the long end from a cast-off row. Use whip stitch (see page 74) to sew the squares together. Because you're sewing up squares, you can match the cast-off stitches of one square to the rows of the next: there'll be 24 stitches or 24 rows to match up. This will keep your blanket even.

This is a versatile design that can be used with any yarn and in many combinations. Use a soft yarn in pastel colours for a baby blanket or make more squares to create a big throw.

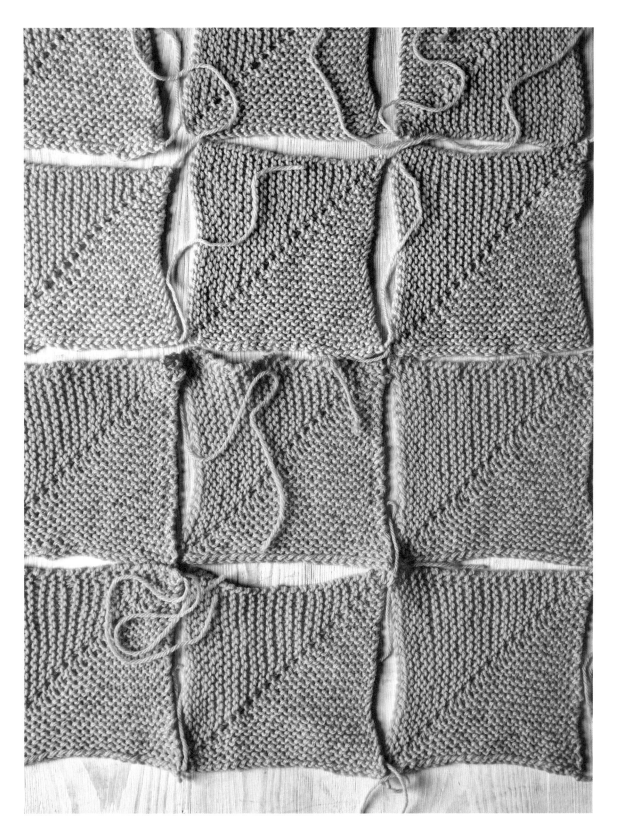

Textured cushion cover

This cushion cover is inspired by the cable patterns of traditional Aran jumpers. Although considerably simpler, it also uses texture to make a very interesting item. In fact, the only technique in this project is using purl stitches on knit rows to create lines of 'wrong side' stitches.

YOU WILL NEED
West Yorkshire Spinners Retreat (or other super chunky yarn): 2 x 100g (140m/153yd) balls in 10 Pure
6.5mm (US 10½) knitting needles
Tapestry needle
40 x 40cm (16 x 16in) cushion pad

SIZE
Approx. 40 x 40cm (16 x 16in)

Cast on 38 stitches.

Rows 1–6: Work in stocking stitch, starting with a knit row.

Row 7: k10, p10, k to end of row.
This is a textured row.

Rows 8–12: Work in stocking stitch, starting with a purl row.

Rows 7–12 set the repeat for the whole project – you'll knit 1 textured row (like row 7) followed by five stocking stitch rows. From now on, the pattern will just include those textured rows; remember, there are five stocking stitch rows between each.

Repeat rows 7–12, with the following variations for the textured row:

Next textured row: k18, p12, k to end of row.

Next textured row: p16, k to end of row.

Next textured row: k20, p14, k to end of row.

Next textured row: k12, p18, k to end of row.

Next textured row: k4, p10, k to end of row.

Next textured row: k14, p12, k to end of row.

Next textured row: k20, p12, k to end of row.

Project continues overleaf

Next textured row: k8, p10, k to end of row.

Next textured row: k20, p18.

Next textured row: k17, p10, k to end of row.

Next textured row: k8, k14, k to end of row.

Next textured row: k14, k12, k to end of row.

Next textured row: k22, p10, k to end of row.
Work five rows in stocking stitch, starting with a purl row.

Cast off.

Repeat for the other side of the cover.

Finishing your cushion cover

Line up the edges and sew together using whip stitch (see page 74) or mattress stitch (see page 76), leaving one side open. Insert the cushion pad and sew the gap closed.

Slouchy beanie

This beanie combines two yarns to create a super-soft and cozy texture. The wool gives the hat some stability and structure and the mohair adds softness and body. You can play with colour by using a contrasting mohair to your wool base. This hat is knitted on circular needles, so you can practise knitting in the round.

YOU WILL NEED

Drops Baby Merino (or other 4-ply merino yarn):
  1 x 50g (175m/191yd) ball in 44 Powder

Drops Kid Silk (or other lace-weight mohair/silk yarn):
  1 x 25g (200m/219yd) ball in 01 Off White

4.5mm (16in) circular needle, 40cm (16in) long

4 x 4.5mm (US 7) double-pointed needles

2 x stitch markers

Tapestry needle

SIZE

Approx. 25 x 20cm (10 x 8in)

Cast on 100 stitches.

It may seem daunting to knit with two yarns at once, but it really is as simple as holding them together. The mohair yarn is fluffy and grips the wool yarn, so they quickly start to behave as though they are from one ball. If you are struggling, you can always substitute a single DK-weight yarn that has the mohair spun in already.

Place a stitch marker to mark the start of your row and join in the round. Make sure your cast-on stitches aren't twisting round your needle. Put a stitch marker after your last cast-on stitch. Put your working needle in your right hand and put it into the very first stitch you cast on. Pull tight and knit the next stitches just as you would if you were knitting flat.

Once you start knitting hats in the round, you'll soon see the advantages over knitting flat and sewing them up! Don't be scared of joining in the round, even if it does seem like a totally different craft.

Knit until the hat measures 20cm (8in), or desired length.

Knit until you reach your stitch marker and slip it from your left to your right needle. You may find that a small gap appears between the first and last stitches of that first row – don't worry, the gap will close up after a row or two. Just knit the next stitch and pull it tight. Simply keep knitting every row, slipping the stitch marker each time you come to it. This hat is designed to use the natural roll of stocking stitch to create a small brim, so there's no ribbing. When you work in the round, you are always working the right side so, to create stocking stitch, you knit every row.

Next row: [k8, k2tog] 10 times.

Once you have reached your desired length, begin the decreases. This hat has 100 stitches, so the decreases are divided into ten sections of ten stitches. Knit eight stitches, then knit two stitches together. Repeat this until the end of the row.

Project continues overleaf

PROJECTS

Next row: [k7, k2tog] 10 times.

Your next row has ten sections of nine stitches, because you've decreased by one stitch per section. So knit seven stitches, then two together, ten times.

Next row: [k6, k2tog] 10 times.

You are now down to ten sections of eight stitches so knit six stitches, then two together, ten times. You will continue to decrease in this way over the next five rows, knitting one less stitch each row before you knit two together. Eventually, your stitches won't stretch around the circular needle so you'll need to switch to double-pointed needles in order to knit this smaller circumference. When this happens, slip your stitches from the circular needle to your double points, distributing the stitches evenly across three needles, with the fourth 'empty' needle being used as your working needle (see pages 54–6).

Next row: [k5, k2tog] 10 times.

Next row: [k4, k2tog] 10 times.

Next row: [k3, k2tog] 10 times.

Next row: [k2, k2tog] 10 times.

Next row: [k1, k2tog] 10 times.

You should have 20 stitches left at the end of this row.

Next row: k2tog to end of row

In your final decrease row there are no knit stitches before the decrease. Knit two stitches together, ten times.

Finishing your beanie

Just like the Chunky Hat with Pompom (see page 104), you will be threading the yarn back through these remaining stitches to secure them. Cut the yarn, leaving a long tail. Thread it onto a tapestry needle and thread it through the next stitch you would work in the round. Continue along the row, sliding the stitches off the knitting needle, and pull tight. Secure this end on the inside of the hat, weaving in the ends (see page 80).

Hot water bottle cover

There's nothing cozier than snuggling up with a hot water bottle. This pattern uses really simple slipped stitches to create texture. It will also help you master working in the round.

YOU WILL NEED
Cascade 220 (or other
   Aran weight yarn):
   1 x 100g (200m/219yd) ball
   in 1001 Living Coral
   1 x 100g (200m/219yd) ball
   in 9694 Raspberry Wine
5mm (US 8) circular needle, 40cm
   (16in) long
5mm (US 8) double-pointed needles
2 x stitch markers
Tapestry needle
2 litre hot water bottle

SIZE
Approx. 33 x 20cm (13 x 8in)

Cast on 64 stitches.
Using a circular needle cast on 64 stitches in Living Coral and join in the round. Place a marker at the beginning of your work and also after 32 stitches, to mark the halfway point.

Round 1: k.

Round 2: [k1, put yarn forward, slip one stitch purlwise, move yarn back, k2] to end of round.
Slipping a stitch purlwise means putting the right needle into the stitch as though you were going to purl – but you just slip it from the left needle without working a new stitch.

Round 3: k.

Round 4: [k3, put yarn forward, slip one stitch purlwise, move yarn back] to end of round.
These four rounds create the semi-woven texture of the project.

Repeat these four rounds until your work measures 22cm (8½in), ending on a plain knit row.

Change to Raspberry Wine.

Continue working in pattern for a further 5cm (2in), until your work measures 27cm (10½in) in total.

Next Round: k1, skk 4 times, k to 9 stitches before marker, k2tog 4 times, k1, slip marker, k1, ssk 4 times, k to 9 stitches before marker, k2tog 4 times (16 stitches decreased).

Project continues overleaf

PROJECTS

Repeat previous round (32 stitches remaining).
Switch to your double-pointed needles.

Next round: [k2, p2] to end of round.
Continue until ribbing measures 6cm (2½in).

Finishing off your hot water bottle cover

Cast off in rib, cut the yarn and weave in all ends except the bottom tail.

Put your hot water bottle into its cover, then sew the bottom edge closed, using the loose yarn tail.

Teddy

Knitting toys is a really lovely thing to be able to do. This bear is simple but makes for a cute first go at making a teddy and would be a lovely gift. It's knitted flat and sewn up afterwards. The instructions below are for the smaller bear, but it's easy to scale up.

YOU WILL NEED

West Yorkshire Spinners Bo Peep
Luxury Baby DK (or other
DK yarn):
1 x 50g (112m/122yd) ball in
431 Treehouse
4mm (US 6) knitting needles
Tapestry needle
Toy stuffing
5mm black button eyes
Black embroidery thread

SIZE

Small bear approx. 10 x 14cm
(4 x 5½in)

BODY

Cast on 9 stitches

Row 1: p.

Row 2: [k1, m1] 8 times, k1.
You're starting at the bottom of the bear's body – this rapid increase row starts its round shape.

Row 3 and all wrong side rows: p.
This instruction tells you to purl every other row – odd-numbered rows will now be omitted from the pattern because you know to purl them.

Row 4: [k2, m1] 8 times, k1.

Row 6: [k3, m1] 8 times, k1.

Row 8: [k4, m1] 8 times, k1.

Row 10: [k5, m1] 8 times, k1.

Row 12: [k6, m1] 8 times, k1.

Row 13: p.

Rows 14–23: Work 10 rows of stocking stitch, starting with a knit row.

Row 24: [k5, k2tog] 8 times, k1.
This decrease row helps with the bear's shaping.

Project continues overleaf

Rows 25–33: Work 9 rows of stocking stitch, starting with a purl row.

Row 34: [k4, k2tog] 8 times, k1.

Rows 35–43: Work 9 rows of stocking stitch, starting with a purl row.

Row 44: [k3, k2tog] 8 times, k1.

Row 46: [k2, k2tog] 8 times, k1.

Row 48: [k1, k2tog] 8 times, k1.

Row 50: [k2tog] 8 times, k1.

Cut the yarn, leaving a long tail. Thread it through the remaining stitches and pull tight. With the end of your yarn, sew the two edges together most of the way. Stuff with toy stuffing, then sew the rest of the body closed. Thread the yarn through the cast-on stitches and pull tight to close up any hole at the bottom. Secure your yarn with a few stitches and trim.

ARMS (MAKE TWO)

Cast on 8 stitches.

Row 1: p.

Row 2: [k1, m1] 7 times, k1.

Rows 3–15: Work in stocking stitch, starting with a purl row.

Row 16: [k2tog] 7 times, k1.
Cut the yarn, leaving a long tail. Thread it through the remaining stitches and pull tight. Sew up the arms, putting a little bit of stuffing inside them, then thread the yarn through the cast-on stitches, just as you did for the body, and pull tight. Sew onto each side of the bear's body in line with the second decrease row.

EARS (MAKE TWO)

Cast on 5 stitches.

Row 1: k.

Row 2: kfb, k3, kfb.
Here you need to increase by knitting first into the front of the stitch on your needle, then into the back of the same stitch (kfb).

Row 3: k.

Row 4: k1, ssk, k1, k2tog, k1.

Row 5: ssk, k1, k2tog.

Cast off.

Finishing your teddy

Sew the ears onto the bear's head using the decreases as a guide to keep them evenly spaced.

Sew the button eyes onto the bear's face very securely and embroider a little nose between them. Have fun giving your bear some personality by playing with the placement of the features!

MAKING A BIGGER BEAR

If you want to make a bigger bear, roughly 15 x 23cm (6 x 9in), follow the same instructions but hold your yarn double and use 6mm (US 10) needles. I used West Yorkshire Spinners Bo Peep Luxury Baby DK in 165 Teddy Bear to make the larger bear.

Shopping bag

Inspired by the classic string bag, this shopper holds plenty of groceries but packs down really tightly. It might seem counterintuitive to drop stitches, but these yarn overs create a loose and lacy texture, coupled only with plain knit stitches.

YOU WILL NEED

Drops Bomull-Lin (or other
   Aran weight cotton/linen yarn):
   2 x 50g balls in 20 Grey Blue
6.5mm (US 10.5) needles
4.5mm (US 7) needles
Tapestry needle
Webbing or fabric tape, for handles
Sewing needle and thread, for
   attaching handles

SIZE

Approx. 30 x 30cm (12 x 12in),
   excluding handles

Cast on 80 stitches.

Knit 6 rows.
These six garter stitch rows form the sturdy top of your bag that the handles will be sewn to.

* Next row: [k1, yon] to last stitch, k1.
This row nearly doubles your stitch count, but don't worry – they disappear in the next row. Once you get into the rhythm of knitting one stitch and wrapping your yarn around your right needle, it won't seem so arduous. Note the asterisk on this instruction – you'll need to return to it later.

Next row: [k1, drop yon] to last stitch, k1.
It seems daunting to drop stitches intentionally but your yarn over needles aren't really stitches – they're a way of adding height to this row. Knit each knitted stitch, then drop the yarn over needle by slipping it off the left needle. The yarn will get 'reabsorbed' by your knit stitches, which will become loose and lacy – perfect for a string shopping bag.

Knit 2 rows.
These knitted rows give some structure to your bag in between the looser rows.

Next row: [k1, yon, yon] to last stitch, k1.
On this row, wrap your yarn around your right needle twice – you'll be dropping these stitches again in the next row, but the double yarn over needles adds even more height to your rows.

Next row: [k1, drop yon, drop yon] to last stitch, k1.
Take your time to make sure you knit the knit stitches and slip the two yarn over needles off your left needle. Giving your knitting a shake or a gentle tug evens out the stitches when you've dropped all the yarn over needles.

Project continues overleaf

Knit 4 rows.
Repeat these ten rows from * twice more. You will have six dropped stitch rows in total.

Switch to 4.5mm needles.
Smaller needles create a denser fabric, which means that the base of your bag will be nice and strong.

Next row: [k8, k2tog] to end of row. (72 sts)
Much like the top of the hat, you are going to decrease every row, in repeated sections of plain knit followed by a decrease. At the end of this row you have decreased by 8 stitches to 72 stitches.

Next row: [k7, k2tog] to end of row. (64 sts)

Next row: [k6, k2tog] to end of row. (56 sts)

Next row: [k5, k2tog] to end of row. (48 sts)

Next row: [k4, k2tog] to end of row. (40 sts)

Next row: [k3, k2tog] to end of row. (32 sts)

Next row: [k2, k2tog] to end of row. (24 sts)

Next row: [k1, k2tog] to end of row. (16 sts)

Next row: [k2tog] to end of row. (8 sts)

Finishing your shopping bag

Cut the yarn, leaving a long tail. Thread it through the remaining stitches and pull tight.

Leave a long enough tail to sew up the side of your bag – it makes it more secure than sewing in a new piece of yarn.

Sew up the side of the bag, keeping your stitches loose on the yarn over rows.

Sew handles onto the band of knit rows at the top of the bag.

Further knitting

WHERE TO FIND PATTERNS

Once you've worked your way through the projects here, you'll want to find new knitting challenges and try new techniques.

Magazine stands are still filled with knitting magazines that commission patterns from top designers. The website Ravelry is a rabbit warren of patterns, projects and inspiration. Users show off their creations for each pattern so you can see how they really knit up. You can lose hours to browsing!

Yarn shops stock both individual patterns and pattern books. Their staff will be able to help you find both the perfect pattern and the yarn to go with it.

YOUR LOCAL YARN SHOP

Yarn shops are fewer and further between than they once were, so if you're lucky enough to have one on your doorstep, make use of it. They'll guide you through your next knitting steps and will have everything you need in one place. Most yarn shops have regular craft meet-ups where you can bring your project and meet other knitters, along with other events and classes to expand your skills.

YARN FESTIVALS

If you really get the bug for knitting, you'll want to visit a yarn festival. These large craft shows are a place for knitters to see new patterns, try new things in workshops and, in all likelihood, pick up a ball of yarn or two. You'll find stalls from both big companies and independent hand-dyers – they're a great chance to spend time around other knitters and see what's happening in the exciting world of knitting.

About the author

Rosie Fletcher is a London-based knitting enthusiast. She owns her own yarn shop and haberdashery called Slipstitch where she runs beginner knitting classes and craft workshops. For more on Rosie, see @slipstitchldn

Acknowledgements

Writing this book has been a dream opportunity and wouldn't have been possible without a whole army of people, only a fraction of whom are mentioned here. Thank you to Odinn for teaching me to knit – the best gift I've ever been given. Thanks to Faith for turning out a whole load of blanket squares and facecloths and for her bottomless well of support. To Rebecca and Yolanda for keeping Slipstitch going when I was hiding in the office with my head in the laptop. To Zena for steering me through my first book, to Caitlin and her amazing illustrations and to Ben, Kim and Rachel for making my knitting look better than it ever has before (and to Kim's kittens for the best photoshoot ever.) To Brenda and Geoffrey for making a dream a reality. To Tim and Caroline and Jessica, with all my love.

Index

acrylic yarn 15, 86
alpaca yarn 15, 118–20
angle scarf project 121–27
Aran weight yarn 12, 108–11,
    121–27, 128–31, 140–43, 148–51

baby shoes project 116–17
ball weight and length 16
beanie project, slouchy 136–39
blanket projects 93, 128–31
brand of yarn 16
broken rib stitch 119–20
bulky weight yarn 12

caring for handknits 86
casting off (CO) 27, 44–45, 53, 57
cast-off edges 45, 53, 74
casting on (CO) 27, 31–32, 50, 54
chunky hat with pompom project
    104–7, 153
chunky scarf project 90–93, 153
chunky weight yarn 12, 112–15
circular needles
    about 19
    how to use 50–53
    projects used in 136–39, 140–43
    sizes 20
    switching to dpns 57, 139, 143
    troubleshooting 57
colour and dye lot 16
colourblock cushion cover project
    98–101

colourwork 16, 60, 61, 63
    projects 98–101, 108–11, 112–15,
        118–20, 121–27, 128–31, 140–43
consistency 74, 100
continental knitting 28–29, 52
cozy project, mug 102–3
cotton yarn 15, 70, 86, 94–97,
    148–51
counting rows 64–65
craft meet-ups 154
cushion cover projects 98–101,
    132–35

decreasing techniques 41–43
    projects used in 104–7, 108–11,
        121–27, 128–31, 136–39,
        140–43, 144–47, 148–51, 153
doorstop project 108–11
double knitting (DK) weight yarn
    12, 63, 94–97, 102–3, 116–17,
    118–20, 144–47
double-pointed needles
    about 19
    how to use 54–56
    projects used in 118–20, 136–39,
        140–43
    sizes 20
    switching from circular needles
        57, 139, 143
    troubleshooting 57
dropped stitches 67, 148–51
drying knitwear 86

ends, sewing/weaving in 22,
    74–81
English vs continental knitting
    28–29, 52
errors, avoiding/fixing *see*
    troubleshooting
extra stitches 68–69
extra yarn over needles 68
eyelets 38, 121–27

facecloths project 94–95
fibre types 15, 16
fingering weight yarn 12
finishing
    hats, closing up 78–79
    mattress stitch 75–76
    pompoms 82–83
    sewing/weaving in ends 22,
        74–81
    tassels 84–85
    whip stitch 74–75
frogging 70

gapping 57
garter stitch 46, 60, 65
    projects used in 94–97, 118–20,
        121–27, 148–51

hats
    closing up 78–79
    pompoms 82–83
    projects 104–7, 136–39, 153
    switching needles 57
headband project 107
holding needles and yarn
    circular needles 50, 52
    double-pointed needles 55, 56
    straight needles 28–29
holding yarn double 63
hot water bottle cover project
    140–43

increasing techniques 38–40
    projects used in 108–11, 121–27,
        144–47

knit front and back (kfb) technique
    40, 144–47
knit (k) stitch 27, 34–35;
    see also projects
knit two together (k2tog) technique
    27, 41
    projects used in 104–7, 108–11,
        121–27, 128–31, 136–39,
        140–43, 144–47, 148–51
knitting first stitch twice 69
knitting on method 27, 31–32,
    50, 54

laceweight yarn 12, 136–39
laddering 57, 67
lifelines 71
light worsted yarn *see* double
    knitting (DK) weight yarn
linen yarn 15, 94–97, 148–51

make 1 stitch (m1) technique 27, 39
    projects used in 108–11, 121–27,
        144–47
mattress stitch 75–76
    projects used in 98–101, 132–35
measuring tape 22
merino yarn 15, 63, 118–20, 136–39
mini cloths project 96–97
mistakes, avoiding/fixing *see*
    troubleshooting
mitred square blanket project
    128–31
mohair yarn 63, 70, 136–39
moss stitch 49
    projects used in 102–3
moths 86
mug cozy project 102–3

name of yarn 16
needles
    attaching yarn to 30
    for casting off 45
    holding 28–29, 50
    size and tension 73
    sizes 20

switching 57
tapestry needles 22, 80
types 19
see also circular needles; double-
    pointed needles; straight
    needles
notions 22

pass slipped stitch over (psso)
    technique 43
patterns, finding 154
patterns, reading 27
plies of yarn 12
pompoms 82–83, 105, 107, 153
projects
    angle scarf 121–27
    baby shoes 116–17
    chunky blanket 93
    chunky hat with pompom
        104–7, 153
    chunky scarf 90–93, 153
    colourblock cushion cover
        98–101
    doorstop 108–11
    headband 107
    hot water bottle cover
        140–43
    mitred square blanket 128–31
    mug cozy 102–3
    reusable face wipes 94–95
    reusable mini cloths 96–97
    shopping bag 148–51
    slouchy beanie 136–39
    tablet case 112–15
    teddy bear 144–47
    textured cushion cover 132–35
    wrist warmers 118–20
purl (p) stitch 27, 36–37;
    see also projects
purl two together (p2tog)
    technique 41
putting stitches back on needle 72

Ravelry website 154
reusable face wipes project

94–95
ribbing 47, 48, 57
    projects used in 90–93, 102–3,
        104–7, 112–15, 118–20, 140–43,
        153
ridges 65
right side (RS) 33, 36
ripping out 70
round, knitting in the
    with circular needles 50–53
    with double-pointed needles
        54–56
    projects used in 118–20, 136–39,
        140–43
    troubleshooting 57
row counters 22, 64, 94
rows 33, 53, 64–65

scarf projects 90–93, 121–27, 153
seams
    mattress stitch 76–77
    whip stitch 74–75
sewing in ends 22, 74–81
shopping bag project 148–51
slip knot 30, 32
slip knit (SSK) technique 27, 42
    projects used in 128–31, 140–43,
        144–47
slipped stitch patterns 62
    projects used in 140–43
Slipstitch haberdashery 154
slouchy beanie project 136–39
splitting a stitch 68
sport weight yarn 12
stitch combinations
    garter stitch 46
    moss stitch 49
    ribbing 48
stitch markers 22, 52, 53, 56, 65,
    70, 140
    projects used in 119, 120, 121,
        128, 136
stitch names and abbreviations
    27
stitches *see specific stitch*

stocking stitch 47, 53, 64, 76–77
   projects used in 94–97, 98–101,
      108–11, 121–27, 132–35,
      136–39, 144–47
straight needles 19, 20, 28–29
   projects used in 90–93, 94–97,
      98–101, 102–3, 104–7, 108–11,
      112–15, 116–17, 121–27, 128–
      31, 132–35, 144–47, 148–51
super bulky/chunky weight yarn
   12, 90–93, 98–101, 104–7, 132–35,
   153
super fine weight yarn 12
switching needles 57

tablet case project 112–15
tapestry needles 22, 74, 80
tassels 84–85, 123, 124, 126
teddy bear project 144–47
tension 28, 73, 80
tension square 73
texture 36, 62–63
   projects 102–3, 118–20, 121–27,
      132–35, 136–39, 140–43
textured cushion cover project
   132–35
tinking 72
troubleshooting
   counting rows 64–65
   dropped stitches 67
   extra stitches 68–69
   extra yarn over needss 68
   knitting in the round 54–56
   knitting first stitch twice 69
   splitting a stitch 68
   twisted stitches 66
tubular knitting *see* round, knitting
   in the
twisted stitches 51, 66

undoing work 70–72

washing handknits 86
weaving in ends 22, 74–81
weight, ball 16

weights, yarn 12
whip stitch 74–75
   projects used in 98–101, 128–31,
      132–35
wool yarn 15, 86, 90–93, 98–101,
   104–7, 118–20, 121–27, 136–39,
   153
worsted weight yarn *see* Aran
   weight yarn
wrist warmers project 118–20
wrong side (WS) 33, 36

yarn
   attaching to needle 30
   fibre types 15; *see also* specific
     type
   holding 28–29, 50
   holding double 63
   joining two balls 60
   plies 12
   reading the yarn band 16
   tension 28, 73, 80
   washing instructions 86
   weights 12; *see also* specific
     weight
yarn festivals 154
yarn over needle (yon) technique
   27, 38
   projects used in 121–27, 148–51
yarn shops 154